a daughter's heart

Overview

A Daughter's Heart: Falling in Love with the Father is based on one conviction: When young women abide with God, everything else falls into place. Perfect for high school or college groups, this six-week Bible study explores the Father's attributes, as well as our response to God's holy, intimate, and loving nature. The format—part Bible study and part devotional—appeals to anyone craving personal, practical, and biblical truth. The approach—energetic and relatable—keeps students interested in several ways:

- Topics are engaging and relevant.
- Devotions/lessons are short but meaty.
- The style is conversational.
- Personal responses enhance discussion and reflection.
- Opportunities for digging deeper appear at the end of each lesson.

Besides its primary use as a small-group Bible study, *A Daughter's Heart* is also perfect for individual devotions. By the end of the book, young women will appreciate just how big their God is and just how much he loves them.

Introductory Session:
Recognizing Where You Are

I can almost see you now, a young woman whose heart overflows with memories, hopes, and disappointments. Is there room for God in there? Christianity *is* a matter of the heart, you know. Think about why you follow God. For some it's practically inevitable since their families are believers. Others study several religions before finding Christianity. For just a minute, consider the driving force behind your faith: Why Jesus and not someone (or something) else? What does having a heart for God mean?

_____

_____

Believe it or not, people can know *about* God but never really know him. Many church members understand the basics, but they've settled for a distant faith, hearing all the Bible stories but never knowing him personally. What a disappointment to God and a disaster for others! His desire—the heart of the matter, really—is an intimate relationship with a devoted daughter.

For a great example of a heart follower, let's look at King David. As you may already know, he wasn't perfect, but at the end of the day, David loved his Lord. Read Psalm 63:1–8 in your Bible. After reading the passage, list any phrases that reveal David's desire for a close relationship with God.

_____

_____

Think about the following questions, writing your answers in the margin if you'd like: When was the last time you desperately needed God? Have you ever told God that his "love is better than life"? Have you shared his love with anyone else?

As this journey of the heart begins, take a moment to consider what you hope to accomplish. Circle any spiritual milestones that excite you:

1. A healthy, biblical understanding of God
2. A personal, enthusiastic relationship with God
3. A practical, clear way to share God's love
4. A sensitive, deliberate concern for others

Think about the current state of your faith. Do you know the heavenly Father? Are you a follower of Jesus Christ? (If you're not sure what I mean, then please read the afterword of this book.) I wonder if your idea of religion centers on rules or dull routines. Or, like David, do you enjoy a loving relationship with God? Evaluate your spiritual health by marking the sentence that best describes you:

_____1. I am learning more about Christianity but haven't yet decided to follow Jesus.

_____2. I am a follower of Jesus, but I don't know very much about him.

_____3. I know a lot about the Bible, but my faith is no more than basic head knowledge.

_____4. I have experienced a close relationship with God before, but it's always been temporary.

_____5. I love God, but I hardly ever talk about him with others.

_____6. I love God and search for opportunities to talk about him with others.

Over the next six weeks, let's get adventurous and ask God to reveal what makes him, well, *God!* When you truly know your Creator, amazing things happen: You begin to look a lot like him, and people notice.

What's Next?

Are you ready to love the Father more intimately than ever? Let's get started! Grab a Bible, this book, a pen, and a quiet place. Each chapter contains five lessons for five days of the week—you choose which days work best. Please tackle just one lesson a day rather than cramming an entire chapter into one sitting. That way, you can think about each topic over a matter of time. Then when your group meets to discuss the chapter you'll be ready.

Oh, how I'd love to witness your deepening love for the Father! Rest assured, though, that I'll be praying for you throughout this study. Now, let's get ready for a heart-changing journey!

Week 1

Comprehending Who He Is

The girls were excited about movie night, an opportunity to hang out with friends after a long week at school. Within fifteen minutes of the opening credits, though, Olivia was uncomfortable. The profanity she heard, coupled with God's name used disrespectfully, made her stomach hurt. How could the actors spew such words without regard to the heavenly Father? What's more, why weren't her Christian friends reacting with the same disgust?

When the name of God is mentioned—reverently or irreverently—what comes to your mind? Some believers, as I'm sure you've noticed, are casual in their attitudes toward the Father. But, to be blunt, they are mistaken. According to the Bible, he is not a vague presence who distantly hovers in the background. Nor is he a genie who exists to grant our every wish. And perhaps most importantly, he is not a weakling who helplessly tolerates the world's disobedience.

Aren't you relieved that he's none of the above? Not only is God in a category all his own, but he created all the categories! This week you'll study five traits that define his unique, wise, and powerful nature. And here's a prediction based on this week's topic: As you begin to appreciate who he is, you'll understand just how beautifully blessed you are.

> I will proclaim the name of the Lord. Oh, praise the greatness of our God! He is the rock, his works are perfect, and all his ways are just. A faithful God who does no wrong, upright and just is he.
>
> Deuteronomy 32:3–4

Day One: Almighty God Is Holy

As you glanced at the title of today's lesson, you may have thought, *Sure, God is holy. I already knew that.* For a few minutes, though, let this truth sink down deep. Picture in your mind a magnificent glow, so pure and white and electric that you don't dare look at it directly. The very presence of this light—God's glory—weakens your knees because even though you are unworthy to approach his throne, the Father invites you. How lovingly and gratefully you bow to him, the one who is pure and majestic. That, daughters of God, is a humbling picture of holiness.

Three Old Testament followers—Moses, Hannah, and Isaiah—experienced God's holiness up close and personal. Read these verses in your Bible, and then summarize each person's thoughts about the Father:

1. Moses's prayer in Exodus 15:11

   God is holy and working wonders

2. Hannah's prayer in 1 Samuel 2:2

   No one is as constant as God // a rock

3. Isaiah's vision in Isaiah 6:3

   God is the holiest

Consider this for a minute: How do you react when you think of Holy God? Here are my responses—circle those that echo yours:

- face to the ground in reverence
- hands to the heavens in praise
- knees bent in humility
- eyes closed in prayerful awe
- tears flowing with gratitude
- mouth singing in worship

How many responses did you circle? Even if you were six for six, here's the potential dilemma: Believers who comprehend the *idea* of holiness sometimes have trouble applying it in everyday life. Place a check beside all the irreverent situations that mock, ignore, or downplay God's holiness:

_✓_1. Displaying a bumper sticker that states, "Jesus is my homeboy."
_✓_2. Squealing, "Oh, my God!" after a surprising experience.
_✓_3. Laughing at a joke that pokes fun at Christianity.
_✓_4. Texting small-talk conversations during a worship service.
_✓_5. Forgetting to give him praise.

As you scanned the list, perhaps other examples of irreverence came to mind. If so, record them here:

_____

_____

Are you surprised at the casual way that Holy God is treated? I'm guilty of at least one example listed above, and you probably saw yourself as well. Here's the deal, though: When we know better, we do better. According to Scripture, God is not a laid-back pal or distant acquaintance that we ignore or take for granted. If there's one part of our lives that deserves reverence, it's the pure nature of God. He is holy. And he requires our highest respect.

We could learn a thing or two about reverence from the Israelites in the Old Testament. Did you know that they rarely spoke God's name because it was too holy for human lips? They spelled it YHWH, an unpronounceable word, choosing instead to call him Lord or Adonai. Even modern-day Jews spell God as G-d since the essence of his name is too holy to write.

How do you feel about the holy nature of God? Are you ready for some awestruck worship? Start by reading Revelation 4:8–11 below, a vision of heaven in which creatures and men declare his holiness. Then make this your prayer to the Father, imagining his glorious throne as you bow at his feet:

Day and night they never stop saying, "Holy, holy, holy is the Lord God Almighty, who was, and is, and is to come." Whenever the living creatures give glory, honor and thanks to him who sits on the throne and who lives forever and ever, the twenty-four elders fall down before him who sits on the throne, and worship him who lives forever and ever. They lay their crowns before the throne and say: "You are worthy, our Lord and God, to receive glory and honor and power, for you created all things, and by your will they were created and have their being."

Revelation 4:8–11

Want to Dig Deeper?

The need for holy daughters is crucial in today's world. You see, God's glory used to reside in manmade structures, but guess where the Holy Spirit lives now? Here's a hint: The New Testament calls our bodies a temple. Read 1 Peter 1:13–16, and write what God says about keeping his dwelling place holy.

Do not conform. Be holy for he is holy. Use self-control Be ready to act.

Stand firm...
Have faith...
He will deliver you.

Day Two: Almighty God Is Jealous

Do you know people who play around with their commitment to God? While they claim that God is important, in reality he barely makes the top ten. Why do you think Christians put other things before God?

_____

_____

I have a theory: Some believers don't realize that God wants to be at the top of every list. Maybe they've never read Deuteronomy 4:39: "Acknowledge and take to heart this day that the Lord is God in heaven above and on the earth below. There is no other."

1. Besides acknowledging God's existence, what else does Deuteronomy 4:39 tell us to do?

_____

_____

2. Write the last sentence of Deuteronomy 4:39.

_____

_____

3. What does this last sentence mean to you?

_____

_____

Exodus 20:5 describes the Father's hatred of misplaced priorities: "I, the Lord your God, am a jealous God." There's no easy way to say this: If you are his child, then he's not kidding around. He loves you and wants to appear at the top of the list. And when you think about it, doesn't he deserve to be?

The truth of the matter, however, is that even devoted daughters get their priorities out of whack. It's called sin, and once we recognize the problem, it's time to repent and turn our eyes toward him. In the Old Testament, Joshua presented this same scenario to some rebellious Israelites. In your Bible, read Joshua 24:19–24.

1. If the people continued rebelling, then what were the consequences (verses 19–20)?

_____

_____

2. What two things did Joshua ask the repentant Israelites to do (verse 23)?

_____

_____

3. What two things did the Israelites promise to do (verse 24)?

_____

_____

Let's do a quick reality check in terms of being faithful: Is God the one you think about? When planning your day-to-day activities, where does he fit? Below, circle his current standing on your list of priorities:

- God is my first thought in the morning.
- God is my focus when I am at church.
- God is my motive for taking care of myself.
- God is my reason for helping others.
- God is my source of guidance and wisdom.

The Father loves us so much that he is jealous of anything we put in front of him! God requires total devotion because he wants what's best for us, and guess what? He is the best. Have you given your whole heart to the one who has always been faithful?

Years ago, I decided that nothing would damage my loving relationship with the Almighty. Do you feel the same? Then let Deuteronomy 6:4–6 be your prayer: "The Lord our God, the Lord is one. Love the Lord your God with all your heart and with all your soul and with all your strength. These commandments that I give you today are to be upon your hearts."

Want to Dig Deeper?

The Ten Commandments, found in Exodus 20, focus on our relationship with God and with others. Read the first four commandments (verses 1–8), and list the ways in which committed believers are faithful to a jealous God.

_____

_____

_____

_____

Day Three: Almighty God Is Unchangeable

While chatting about her favorite Old Testament adventures, one of my students wished she had lived when God's superpowers, as she called them, were undeniable. "He parted seas and made donkeys talk!" she exclaimed. "Nowadays, God isn't involved. He's mostly laid-back and a whole lot harder to find."

"Are you kidding?" I wanted to say. "You think God is extinct?" Instead, I began sharing a few miracles from my own life, and pretty soon this precious teen realized that he still shows up, Old Testament style, in the lives of his children. Without a doubt, we serve the very same Lord that Moses and Balaam encountered. But don't take my word for it. Read these passages from the book of truth:

- "I the Lord do not change" (Malachi 3:6).
- "Jesus Christ is the same yesterday and today and forever" (Hebrews 13:8).
- "Every good and perfect gift is from above, coming down from the Father of the heavenly lights, who does not change like shifting shadows" (James 1:17).

1. What is the common theme running through these verses?

_____

_____

2. Why do you think God performed so many miracles in the Old Testament?

_____

_____

3. What are some New Testament miracles that come to mind?

_____

_____

Sometimes it's hard to imagine that the same God who spoke to Moses is the same one who guides us. But he is. Oh, the method of delivery may be different, but don't be fooled into thinking that today's still, small voice is weaker, more tolerant, or more distant. Satan would love for you to view the Lord as nothing more than an out-of-date grandfather hanging out on a cloud. Big mistake.

Believe it or not, God is just as involved with us now as he was with the ancient heroes. Aren't you relieved to know that his character is the same? In your Bible, read these verses, and then list God's traits that last forever:

1. Deuteronomy 33:27

_____

_____

2. Psalm 103:17

_____

_____

3. Isaiah 54:8

_____

_____

What a relief to know that the things every young woman craves—protection, love, and acceptance—are available to you, courtesy of Almighty God! Do you feel them? Even if you don't, those invisible arms are indeed there, holding you tight.

From experience, let me encourage you with this: The more you know him, the more you'll feel God's awesome and unchangeable nature. Below, check the ways you've witnessed these "superpowers" of God:

_____1. God's power through nature
_____2. God's power through healing
_____3. God's protection of your physical body
_____4. God's protection of your thoughts
_____5. God's answer to a specific spiritual question
_____6. God's guidance over a life-changing decision

Feel free to explain your answers or to add other experiences not found on the list:

_____

_____

Thank goodness for an unchangeable God! In your prayer time, let him know the eternal traits you appreciate. Then repeat the following verses as praise to your holy, jealous, and unchangeable Father: "You, O Lord, sit enthroned forever; your renown endures through all generations. But you remain the same, and your years will never end" (Psalm 102:12, 27).

Want to Dig Deeper?

A fancy word for God's unchanging nature is *immutability*. How wonderful that we can enjoy his immutability forever! What does he promise us in John 14:1–4 and 2 Peter 1:11?

_____

_____

_____

_____

Day Four: Almighty God Is All-Knowing

Today's lesson might stretch your brain since the topic can go in circles. Are you ready? God is omniscient, as 1 John 3:20 reveals, and that means he sees bad news coming your way. So if he is capable, as the Bible states, then why doesn't he stop it? Here's another one: Following him is your choice, a concept known as free will, but God already knows each decision you'll make. Perhaps the biggest mind bender of all has to do with prayer: Although he realizes your request before it's uttered, God wants you to ask him anyway. What an unexplainable Father! What are some other mysteries that make your head swim?

_____

_____

Even though I don't always understand God's wisdom, over time it's become easier to accept. You see, for years he has been my faithful Lord. Without a doubt, he's transformed my heart. He's also guided me through troubled times, shielding me from harm. Basically, after witnessing the presence of God, I'd be foolish to stumble over the details! And scripturally, we aren't supposed to understand every part of him, as Deuteronomy 29:29 reveals: "The secret things belong to the Lord...."

Even though we don't comprehend his ways, isn't it comforting to bring our concerns to God? We simply need to approach him honestly and often. Read these verses, and answer the questions that follow:

- "A man's ways are in full view of the Lord, and he examines all his paths" (Proverbs 5:21).
- "... your Father knows what you need before you ask him" (Matthew 6:8).

1. What does God see behind the scenes when you're considering a certain decision?

_____

_____

2. Why does God sometimes say no when you ask for something specific?

_____

_____

3. Why are these verses comforting to you?

_____

_____

I've always been amazed at the personal attention our Father gives his children. He could lump us all together, you know, and treat us like a bunch of whining, rebellious misfits. But he doesn't. In your Bible, read Psalm 139:1–4, and list all the personal details that God specifically sees:

1. He knows when I _____.

2. He can read my _____.

3. He is familiar with all of my _____.

4. He knows every _____.

God knows it all, so he's the logical source for guidance. He knows what's coming along your path, and he knows what you'll need for the challenge. Have you ever noticed the way he prepares you for the future? Maybe he alerts you to the perfect Bible verse, or perhaps he gives you strength for a tough situation. The relief of serving an omniscient God is obvious: Following him today guarantees you'll be in great shape tomorrow—no worries, no regrets, and no doubts. No kidding!

Do you want to become the spiritual giant you're supposed to be? It starts with clinging to an all-knowing God and embracing his all-knowing plan:

> "I know the plans I have for you," declares the Lord, "plans to prosper you and not to harm you, plans to give you hope and a future. Then you will call upon me and come and pray to me, and I will listen to you. You will seek me and find me when you seek me with all your heart."
>
> Jeremiah 29:11–13

Want to Dig Deeper?

One Sunday during Bible study, the room was filled with complaining students. They continued to moan until the teacher uttered a startling truth: "Ladies, this world is not perfect, and God does not need your approval. In fact, he can do whatever he wants. If you'll remember, he is God." Ouch. Yes, God is sovereign, and we are not. Read these verses, and then write a prayerful praise to God acknowledging his omniscience:

- Psalm 103:19
- Romans 11:33–36

_____

_____

_____

_____

Day Five: Almighty God Is Love

Why does Almighty God persistently woo you? Why does he protect you? And bless you? In a nutshell, it all comes down to love. The creation *of* you, the sacrifice *for* you, and the victory promised *to* you—it's all because of love. That's just who he is, as 1 John 4:16 states. God is love. Love is God. Simply put, one cannot exist without the other.

If you've been a church member for very long, then you've heard this truth pretty often. Today, though, I hope you'll see with fresh eyes the creator's adoration of y-o-u! Let's start with a quick review of his love, according to God. Circle any phrases that are especially meaningful:

1. When I'm uncertain: "In your unfailing love you will lead the people you have redeemed" (Exodus 15:13).
2. What I've been given: "Remember, O Lord, your great mercy and love, for they are from of old" (Psalm 25:6).
3. When I'm disciplined: "...do not despise the Lord's discipline and do not resent his rebuke, because the Lord disciplines those he loves..." (Proverbs 3:11–12).
4. Why I need his love: "But God demonstrates his own love for us in this: While we were still sinners, Christ died for us" (Romans 5:8).
5. Where I'll spend eternity: "Because of his great love for us, God, who is rich in mercy, made us alive with Christ even when we were dead in transgressions—it is by grace you have been saved" (Ephesians 2:4–5).

Because God is love and we desperately want acceptance, can you imagine people rejecting him? But they do, don't they? As I write these words, someone close to me has turned her back on the Father. Out of rebellion or immaturity, she has chosen to "take a break from God and try other things." What a foolish, costly, and selfish decision! Does she not understand the depth of love available to her? Does she not realize that disobedience breaks his heart? Why do you think that people like my friend willingly reject the Father?

In my own life, when I've neglected the Father's love, God has mercifully returned me to the fold. What a comforting reminder as I gently guide my friend toward forgiveness! As I pray for her, there is such relief in these verses about God's beautiful persistence:

- "What do you think? If a man owns a hundred sheep, and one of them wanders away, will he not leave the ninety-nine on the hills and go to look for the one that wandered off?" (Matthew 18:12).
- "[Jesus said] As the Father has loved me, so have I loved you. Now remain in my love.... You did not choose me, but I chose you ..." (John 15:9, 16).

1. Why do you think God spends so much energy on a child who is off track?

_____

_____

2. Why does Jesus, God's son, love you?

_____

_____

3. Who chooses whom when it comes to your relationship with the Father?

_____

_____

If you think about it, the entire Bible is one long love letter from God to us. Starting with Genesis, when he walked with Adam, and ending in Revelation, when he welcomes us into heaven, the common thread is love. And halfway through is Jesus, the one who made us worthy: "For God so loved the world, that he gave his one and only son, that whoever believes in him shall not perish but have eternal life" (John 3:16).

Can any of us truly comprehend God's love? I pray that this truth becomes more precious each day. Oh, that our words and actions would share it with others! If you, like me, have experienced it firsthand, then why not thank the Father for his deep, continuous love? Better yet, why not pray for those who've yet to embrace it?

Want to Dig Deeper?

God is love, but he does not love everything, as Amos 5:15 and Malachi 2:16 reveal. Read both verses and summarize below:

_____

_____

_____

_____

Week 2

Appreciating What He Did

When I received a cross necklace for my birthday, I couldn't wait to show it off. So imagine my horror when someone asked, "How could you advertise a cruel God who sacrificed his innocent son?" I just sat there, shocked, before realizing that this lady didn't know the whole story, the one about a God who loved the entire world enough to do an unthinkable thing.

"Well," I replied, "this cross reminds me of hope. Yes, God's Son was killed there, but he did it willingly, just as his Father asked. The best part, though, is that Jesus is alive today with God in heaven, and I will join them someday." Ever since that conversation, I've looked at the cross differently. It is indeed a wonderful yet misunderstood symbol, isn't it?

Jesus's death, we must remember, was no surprise to his Father. This was God's long-term plan, one that required his own perfect Son as an offering. Who else but a loving and unselfish Father could allow this? More than anything, he desired an intimate relationship with the children he'd created, a bond that sin couldn't break. So God did what had to be done, all for me. And for you.

This week we'll examine how Jesus, while on earth, obeyed the Father's plan to fill our greatest needs. For three years, he showed us how to serve. For forty days, he showed us how to hope. And in between—during those six hours of torture—he showed us the way to the Father.

> Jesus said to them, "If God were your Father, you would love me, for I came from God and now am here. I have not come on my own, but he sent me."
>
> John 8:42

Day One: The Son of God Lived as a Man

You've probably heard all about Jesus's thirty-three-year visit to earth, an adventure that included a virgin birth, unjust crucifixion, and victorious resurrection. Have you considered, though, how degrading it must have been for God's Son to put on a "human suit"? Day in and day out, Jesus Christ also faced the struggles we encounter. Yes, he was completely holy, but he was also completely human, surrounded by heartache, injustice, and sin.

Does it break your heart that God's Son was given less than the royal treatment? I guess it all started when a perfect baby took his first little breath among the livestock. Then when he was barely out of the stable, Jesus became a fugitive, moving from one place to another as King Herod hunted him down. And as you probably know, the trials got much worse. In his thirties, when God instructed him to claim a new promise, the tide soon turned horribly. Read these verses about Jesus's earthly experience, and then reflect on several questions:

- "He was despised and rejected by men, a man of sorrows, and familiar with suffering. Like one from whom men hide their faces, he was despised, and we esteemed him not" (Isaiah 53:3).
- "He was in the world, and though the world was made through him, the world did not recognize him" (John 1:10).

1. As Jesus poured out his message from the Father, how was he treated?

_____

_____

2. When have you rejected or ignored God's Son in your own life?

_____

_____

3. Have people ever treated you badly because of your faith in God? If you feel comfortable, describe a time when you or someone you know experienced persecution.

_____

_____

There's no doubt about it: Doing the right thing—God's plan—is tough when people treat you unfairly. But when rejection comes, just remember that your Father's approval is all that matters. Let God's instruction and influence shine, no matter what, just like Jesus did. Read 1 John 1:14: "The Word became flesh and made his dwelling among us. We have seen his glory, the glory of the one and only, who came from the Father, full of grace and truth."

1. What did people see when they were around Jesus?

_____

_____

2. How can you show God's glory to the people around you?

_____

_____

The day-to-day example that Christ offered should change our lives as well. Do you sometimes view those "Jesus tales" as entertaining stories for kids? Well, they're not—everything that's recorded is an adult-sized manual for hurting, doubting, and complaining people. In your Bible, find these verses to see exactly how Jesus shared his Father with a dying world:

1. In Mark 1:38, Jesus came to earth so that he could

   _____.

2. In John 12:46, Jesus came into the world as a

   _____.

3. In John 18:37, Jesus came to tell everyone the

   _____.

Before Jesus died, he showed us how to live. He realizes that it's difficult and exhausting—he was here too, remember? But Jesus also knows that this world desperately needs the Father's love. He's shown it to you at great cost. Will you show it to others? Spend some time today thanking God for sending his perfect Son to this imperfect earth. Then pray about the example you show to others, asking the Father to reveal his undeniable presence.

Want to Dig Deeper?

Just after Jesus began his ministry, the Holy Spirit sent him to the desert for an experience with temptation. Read Matthew 4:1–11, and write the three ways in which Jesus was tempted. Also note what happened when he resisted the third time.

_____

_____

_____

_____

Day Two: The Son of God Died on a Cross

Little kids at church know all about Jesus on the cross. There's usually no emotion as they tell the story, simply because they're too young to grasp the horror of it. Unfortunately, though, lots of older Christians are also unaffected about the day God's Son died. Maybe they're spiritually immature. Or perhaps they've never considered their own involvement in the sacrifice. Some probably think that Jesus's death was no big deal for the powerful Son of God.

Do you realize, though, that Jesus begged his Father for Plan B? That obeying God's will for crucifixion was a monumental struggle? Yes, Jesus understood the reason for dying and accepted it, but don't ever assume that his mission was easy:

- "[Jesus said] Now my heart is troubled, and what shall I say? 'Father, save me from this hour'? No, it was for this very reason I came to this hour. Father, glorify your name" (John 12:27–28)!
- "[Jesus said] 'Father, if you are willing, take this cup from me; yet not my will, but yours be done.' An angel from heaven appeared to him and strengthened him. And being in anguish, he prayed more earnestly, and his sweat was like drops of blood falling to the ground" (Luke 22:42–44).

1. How did Jesus show his reluctance to die on a cross?

_____

_____

2. How do you suppose God reacted when Jesus begged for another way?

_____

_____

3. What part of Jesus's death do you think was most horrifying to both the Father and the Son?

_____

_____

Before Jesus came to earth, people tried lots of ways to become pure and pleasing to God—sacrificing animals and obeying tons of rules, for starters—but they failed to follow through. And when they failed, those ugly sins remained, the ones separating them from the Father. So Jesus stepped in, offering himself as a one-time payment for all. No more sacrifices, no more rules. Just the pure blood of Jesus Christ, just as God planned. In your Bible, find Ephesians 5:2.

1. What did the (figurative) smoke of Christ's sacrifice smell like to God?

_____

_____

2. Why was Jesus's blood a fragrant offering to God Almighty?

_____

_____

3. Why did Jesus give his life for you?

_____

_____

All this suffering—the crown of thorns, the mocking, the separation from God—happened to an innocent man who felt every painful prick, sarcastic comment, and dark hopelessness. And it happened for one reason—so that you could know your Father intimately, both in this life and in the next. This is how much Holy God loves you; he gave his only Son.

Sadly, I was in my twenties before the reality of Jesus's suffering set in. His death on my behalf was such a precious gift that I took for granted. What about you? Look at the following list, and draw a cross beside the amount of gratitude you *should* offer God for Christ's death. Then write your initials beside the amount of gratitude you typically show:

1. I never thank God for or even think about Christ's death.
2. I sometimes remember to thank God for Christ's death.
3. I often feel gratitude for Christ's death.
4. I always show gratitude for Christ's death.

I don't know about you, but I am so thankful that God took care of my sins two thousand years ago! Because of his ultimate offering, I am clean before the Lord. How can I possibly express my joy over this life-changing event? Like me, are you on your knees in gratitude? Let's thank our Father for the freedom we enjoy, all because of a terrible, necessary, love-filled cross.

Want to Dig Deeper?

Long before Jesus was born, Isaiah wrote in detail about the crucifixion. Read his account in Isaiah 53:5–10, and list the events that were recorded long before the first Good Friday.

_____

_____

_____

_____

Day Three: The Son of God Rose from the Dead

If you could personally live out one scene from the Bible, which would you choose? A sea parting in the middle so that panicked Israelites could cross? A crowd of people feasting on bread and fish? Or a quiet tomb on a certain Sunday morning? Hands down, I would choose the happiest day on earth: Jesus Christ, the human sacrifice, kicked Satan in the face with a holy reappearance. Christ had told the truth all along, and he was miraculously alive! Circle the emotions you might have felt if you'd found an empty tomb:

> Fear
> Anger
> Depression
> Excitement
> Peace
> Panic
> Confusion
> Awe

Let's see how two primary visitors, Mary Magdalene and James's mother, Mary, reacted:

- "The women hurried away from the tomb, afraid yet filled with joy, and ran to tell his disciples" (Matthew 28:8).
- "Trembling and bewildered, the women went out and fled from the tomb" (Mark 16:8).
- "While they were wondering about this, suddenly two men in clothes that gleamed like lightning stood beside them. In their fright the women bowed down with their faces to the ground, but the men said to them, 'Why do you look for the living among the dead?'" (Luke 24:4–5).

They were paralyzed with fright, weren't they? Why? Didn't they remember Jesus saying that he'd rise again on the third day? Couldn't they count? Before we're too hard on them, though, let's put ourselves in the same situation. They had just experienced the trauma of seeing their Savior on a cross. They'd probably lost sleep and appetites. Almost certainly, they'd never seen the white-lightning glory of God before now. And their plans were suddenly switched from visiting a tomb to celebrating a ghost. Here's a question: How do you think their lives were changed after witnessing this Sunday morning miracle?

Here's a more personal question: Is the resurrection story a crucial part of *your* experience? It better be, or your faith is like every other religion, worshiping a dead man who left rules, not empty tombs. Like the overwhelmed Marys discovered, Christ's resurrection was not only an exciting event but also a necessary one. In your Bible, read 1 Corinthians 15: 14–17.

1. If Christ had not been resurrected, then our faith would be _____ (verse 14).

2. If Christ had not been resurrected, then we would be _____ (verse 15).

3. If Christ had not been resurrected, then we would still live in our _____ (verse 17).

Make no mistake: The cross rescued us from sin's punishment. But the empty tomb—the one that stirred up rumors of a stolen body and hallucinating witnesses—helped us know, once and for all, that God's promise was victoriously fulfilled. Satan's schemes had failed. And Jesus's words were absolutely true: "The angel said to the women, 'Do not be afraid, for I know that you are looking for Jesus, who was crucified. He is not here; he has risen, just as he said ... '" (Matthew 28:5–6).

Do you awake each morning expecting to hear from the risen Lord? Are you convinced that he keeps his word? Or, like the Sunday morning Marys, have you forgotten his promise to stick around? He is alive and well, you know, and has big plans for daughters who celebrate an empty tomb: "Then Jesus told him, 'Because you have seen me, you have believed; blessed are those who have not seen and yet have believed'" (John 20:29).

Want to Dig Deeper?

After Jesus arose from the dead, many followers did not recognize him. Read one account in Luke 24:13–35. Why do you think people walked alongside the Son of God but did not realize his identity?

_____

_____

_____

_____

Day Four: The Son of God Ascended to Heaven

A college student recently asked, "When Jesus came out of that tomb, why didn't he return to heaven right then? And how did he get back to heaven, anyway?" I was just about to answer when another student argued that these questions were irrelevant. All that mattered, she continued, was that Jesus was "up there" now, at the right hand of God.

What do *you* think? Are the specifics of Jesus's life after his resurrection, including his return to heaven, important? List what you already know about Jesus's activities between that first Easter morning and his return to the Father:

_____

_____

After Jesus was killed and then resurrected, he still had some earthly work to do. For forty days after he came out of that tomb, Christ—with a glorious, resurrected body—stuck around for several reasons. In your Bible, read Acts 1:3–5, and circle all the activities he focused on during those forty days:

Discussed the Holy Spirit
Found more disciples
Got revenge
Proved he was alive
Rebuilt the temple
Talked about heaven

Just think: Christ, the one who suffered so unfairly, chose to hang around for a little while longer. Wouldn't *you* have wanted to blink your eyes and make earth a distant memory? Not Jesus. Before returning to the right hand of God, Christ had a few items on the to-do list: proving his victory over death (what excitement!), explaining the hope of heaven (what anticipation!), and promising the Holy Spirit (what power!).

And then, after forty days, it was time for the big departure. Would you assume that the send-off was loud and dramatic or quiet and peaceful? Do you think that Jesus's followers were happy or heartbroken? Read these verses to see exactly how it happened:

- "[Jesus] lifted up his hands and blessed them. While he was blessing them, he left them and was taken up into heaven. Then they worshiped him and returned to Jerusalem with great joy" (Luke 24:50–52).

- "After he said this, he was taken up before their very eyes, and a cloud hid him from their sight. They were looking intently up into the sky as he was going, when suddenly two men dressed in white stood beside them. 'Men of Galilee,' they said, 'Why do you stand here looking into the sky? This same Jesus, who has been taken from you into heaven, will come back in the same way you have seen him go into heaven'" (Acts 1:9–11).

Place a check beside the statements you find particularly interesting:

_____1. Jesus taught his followers until the very last moment of his time on earth.

_____2. His followers were joyful as Jesus returned to heaven.

_____3. His followers actually saw Jesus rising from earth, disappearing into the clouds.

_____4. Two angels appeared as Jesus was leaving earth.

_____5. His entrance into heaven showed us the way he'll return to earth.

The fact that Jesus's followers were joyful at the departure always catches me by surprise. I would have pictured the scene with many tears and heavy hearts. But maybe a miracle like this was just what their traumatized hearts needed to see—instead of looking up to remember him suffering on a cross, there he was, alive and glorious, floating toward his Father. Wow. After witnessing something like this, it was easy to believe that he would indeed return, *this* time as the king that everyone would worship.

He will come back, you know. Today let's thank him specifically for that faith-building transfer from earth to heaven. And then let's thank him for the eventual, victorious return to earth. As his child, aren't you excited about seeing the Son? And kneeling at the throne of the Father? Sometimes I don't think I can wait!

Want to Dig Deeper?

When Jesus ascended to heaven, he didn't abandon believers. Instead, the third part of the trinity, the Holy Spirit, came to unleash the power of God. Read about Jesus's promise of the Holy Spirit in these verses:

- Read John 14:15–18 to learn where the Holy Spirit lives.
- Read Acts 1:7–8 to understand why the Holy Spirit's power exists.

Day Five: The Son of God Is Coming Back

Sometimes, when the horizon bursts with color and sunshine peeks through the clouds, I can almost picture Jesus making his entrance. In my mind, he covers the entire sky and glows with white-hot light. And he's on a mission: Finally, after being cursed, doubted, and ignored, the King of kings is coming to set the record straight.

This event, often called the "second coming," is actually going to happen. Maybe not exactly as I imagine it, but the Bible is clear that one day—and no one but God knows exactly when—Jesus Christ will return to earth as a mighty king. Does this thought excite you as much as it excites me? If you're on his winning team, then I'll bet you're ecstatic! Read these verses about the triumphant second coming:

- "At that time the sign of the Son of Man will appear in the sky, and all the nations of the earth will mourn. They will see the Son of Man coming on the clouds of the sky, with power and great glory" (Matthew 24:30).
- "I saw heaven standing open and there before me was a white horse, whose rider is called Faithful and True. With justice he judges and makes war. His eyes are like blazing fire, and on his head are many crowns" (Revelation 19:11–12).

1. Why will nations become sorrowful when they realize that Jesus (the Son of Man) is coming?

_____

_____

2. What does Jesus (the Son of Man) look like?

_____

_____

3. How do you think people will react when they see him coming?

_____

_____

Before we go any further, let's talk a little about some end-of-the-world matters. First, there's a lot that we don't understand (and apparently that's just fine since God didn't choose to spell out everything). Second, believers may interpret the order of events a bit differently, but no worries here: For this particular discussion, we'll stick to clear-cut, common ground. Are you ready? Let's slowly dip our toe into the second coming pool.

At some point—when the world as we know it will change forever—the Father will instruct Christ to return to earth, defeat evil, and create a kingdom of justice and peace. How do you feel about the promise of the second coming? Check all the statements that express your thoughts:

_____1. I am afraid because I'm not sure that I am God's daughter. What will happen to me?

_____2. I am afraid because people I love are not God's children. What will happen to them?

_____3. I am excited because I am sure that I am God's daughter. He will take care of me.

_____4. I am excited because good will finally win, and Satan will lose his power.

Use this space to express any other thoughts about the second coming, as well as questions you may have.

_____

_____

_____

_____

When thinking about Christ's return, some believers are anxious. Others are confused. There's no need, though. The same Father who loves you, protects you, and guides you will direct the one stepping out of the sky. You trust both of them, right? Then why be apprehensive? Find the following verses in your Bible to understand these optimistic promises:

1. John 14:2–3 says that God's Son will take care of you: "I am going to prepare a place for you. And if I go and prepare a place for you, I will _____ _____ and take you to be with me...."

2. Revelation 22:7 promises that God's Son will reward you: "Behold, I am coming soon! _____ is he who keeps the words of the prophecy in this book."

3. Revelation 19:15–16 says that God's Son will fight for justice: "Out of his mouth comes a sharp sword with which to strike down the nations. He will rule them with an iron scepter … On his robe and on his thigh he has this name written: King of_____ and Lord of _____."

As a follower of God in a messed-up world, I hope you are comforted by the end of the story. The Father is in control, and his plan includes a wonderful future! Today, praise him for defeating evil and taking care of you. Consider praying the words of Titus 2:13 aloud as a confident vote of faith: "We wait for the blessed hope—the glorious appearing of our great God and Savior, Jesus Christ." Amen!

Want to Dig Deeper?

Even though there is mystery surrounding what's called "end times," we can get a partial picture from Scripture. Read these verses to gather a few details:

- Matthew 24:36–44
- 1 Corinthians 15:51–52
- 1 Thessalonians 4:16–18

1. After reading these verses, what did you learn about end times?

_____

_____

2. After reading these verses, what questions are raised?

_____

_____

3. Why should believers live without fear of Christ's return, even if they don't understand all the details?

_____

_____

Week 3

Embracing What He Promises

Courtney was only four, but she loved to sing. By sing, I mean that at any given time she might belt out a Christmas carol or Disney song. Her favorite hobby, though, was creating original love songs to God. One day, after lots of coaxing from her mom, Courtney shared with me her latest creation (the tune was much like "Happy Birthday," if you'd like to hum along): "God promises lots. God promises lots. He loves me; I love him; God promises lots." Amen, sweet Courtney! I have a feeling that when these precious words reached heaven, angels sang along.

How often do you sing the truth of God's promises? When you do, I hope the main verse celebrates a biggie—eternity with God—since that's the one that really counts. There are other verses, though, that praise his vow to stay close during trouble. Corrie Ten Boom, a Holocaust survivor, perhaps said it best: "Let God's promises shine in your problems." Are you living with conflict? Fear? According to Scripture, God not only guides you through every situation but does it with the comforting peace of his presence. And that's a promise I can sing from experience.

> His divine power has given us everything we need for life and godliness through our knowledge of him who called us by his own glory and goodness. Through these he has given us his very great and precious promises, so that through them you may participate in the divine nature and escape the corruption in the world caused by evil desires.
>
> 2 Peter 1:3–4

Day One: The Holy One Assures His Presence

During one of the darkest nights of my life, I was face down on the floor, shaking with sobs. Terrible news had come, and it was overwhelming. Even then, before family and friends swooped in with hugs and casseroles, someone was there with me. How could I know for sure? How can anyone possibly explain the presence of an invisible God? Inside my heart, though, I sensed hope in the midst of sadness; inside my head, I heard scriptures that offered comfort; and inside my spirit, I felt strong arms that never, ever let me go.

He is there, sweet daughter of God. No matter who you are, no matter what you've done, and no matter where you're going, the Father plants himself right where you are. And that's an empowering promise. Look at these verses about your ever-present God:

- "Be strong and courageous. Do not be afraid or terrified, for the Lord your God goes with you; He will never leave you nor forsake you" (Deuteronomy 31:6).
- "By day the Lord directs his love, at night his song is with me—a prayer to the God of my life" (Psalm 42:8).

1. When have you felt afraid? Were you aware of God's presence during a scary time? If so, then how?

_____

_____

2. How does God show his undeniable presence to the author of Psalm 42?

_____

_____

In my own life, there have been times when I couldn't sense the presence of God. But make no mistake: If you are his child, then God is there, period. He never said, "I'll be there unless something comes up" or "If you need me, let me know." In Matthew 28:20, his Son, Jesus, vows to stay close until the end of time, and that's regardless of your emotions, shortcomings, or circumstances. But even though you're aware of this promise, have you ever felt that the Father was distant? If so, then circle the possible reasons for this false sense of alienation:

Absence of intimate prayer time
Absence of regular Bible study
Misplaced priorities
Poor earthly example of a father
Questions that caused doubt
Rebellion/sin
Tragedy
Withdrawal from church or Christian friends

When I question God's promise to be near, it's usually time for some self-reflection: Is sin keeping me from an intimate relationship? Am I neglecting quality time with him? Are the world's views about the Father creeping into my thoughts? As one old preacher used to say, "God is always in the same place, close by. If you don't feel him, then guess who's changed locations." Read these verses, and list the keys to sensing God's intimate presence:

• Jeremiah 29:12–13
    1. _____ on God.
    2. _____ God with all your heart.

• James 4:7–8
    1. _____ yourself to God.
    2. _____ the devil.
    3. _____ near to God.

The relief of knowing I'm not alone is such a comforting promise! This stressful world is full of problems, but thankfully I can face them with a not-so-secret weapon: God; he is present, involved, and committed to sticking around. Are you embracing this beautiful promise? Today, thank the Father for his presence, and consider practical ways to keep your relationship with him consistently close.

Want to Dig Deeper?

Sometimes, even for those who seek him, God seems silent. A perfect example is Job, a godly man who listened but for a while heard nothing. Was God absent? No. Was he at work behind the scenes? Absolutely. By the end of Job's trial, we see a more mature believer who realized God's faithfulness. Below, place a check beside the ways you can grow during times of silence:

____ dependence (relying solely on God)
____ faith (trusting when you don't see)
____ friendships (sharing your needs with godly believers)
____ knowledge (searching the Scriptures for truth)
____ prayer (voicing your concerns to the Father)

Day Two: The Holy One Ensures Peace

A friend of mine was having a meltdown—there's no other way to describe it—so I grabbed my Bible, hoping to read her some comforting verses. She wasn't feeling it, though. "I know God promises to give me peace!" she said. "But what good does it do if I don't *feel* it?" Good point, wouldn't you say? How would you have responded to my friend if given the chance?

After I gathered my thoughts, something like this came out of my mouth: "You *can* feel peace if you want. It's right in front of you. Just focus on him and it'll happen, guaranteed." Do you agree that the supernatural peace of God is simple to access? Is it really possible to let go of paralyzing anxiety? According to the Bible, yes!

- "In Christ Jesus you who once were far away have been brought near through the blood of Christ. For he himself is our peace…" (Ephesians 2:13–14).
- "Let the peace of Christ rule in your hearts, since as members of one body you were called to peace. And be thankful" (Colossians 3:15).

Answer True or False for the following statements.

1. ____ Christ's sacrifice made it possible for me to experience peace.
2. ____ The peace of Christ should consume my whole being.
3. ____ If I have Christ in my heart, then I have access to peace.
4. ____ When I am consciously thankful, my outlook is peaceful.
5. ____ Constant worry suggests that I'm not trusting God to take care of me.

Did you mark "true" for each statement? If so, then congratulations; you're on the way to a peaceful existence! If you're a follower of God, then you already know where to look for answers: Focus on him. First Peter 3:11 states, "Seek peace; pursue it." And you can find it by daily proclaiming that he is your peace. Then you can enjoy it by reminding yourself, through quiet times with the Father, that he is in control.

In which areas of your life do you struggle with feelings of worry? Rank the following categories from 1–8, with 1 being the most stressful:

_____ body issues
_____ dating/guys
_____ family
_____ friends
_____ future
_____ health
_____ money
_____ school/career

When a daughter claims God's peace, she enjoys inner calm and security. Remember, though, that outside circumstances may still be chaotic. In fact, a quick look at the disciples' journey shows that things could get *worse* after claiming the promise. But if this happens, so what? Whatever kind of nutty circus is around you, a follower of God can rest easy. Read Philippians 4:4–9 in your Bible. (Oh, and you might want to underline these powerful words about peace; they are some of my favorites.)

1. Instead of being anxious, what should you consciously do instead?

_____

_____

2. Even though it's tough to comprehend, what happens when you give every problem to God?

_____

_____

3. What kinds of thoughts are important to enjoying the Father's peace?

_____

_____

Experiencing peace is really as simple as thinking about the goodness of God. Jesus Christ did the hard work of providing the way. Why not thank him today for the calming assurance of the cross?

Want to Dig Deeper?

God promises peace, and then he expects you to share it with others. What do the following verses say about the Christian's commitment to peaceful living?

- Matthew 5:9
- Titus 3:2

_____

_____

_____

_____

Day Three: The Holy One Reveals Wisdom

How confident are you when it comes to making those big decisions about school, careers, or relationships? What about the smaller ones, like whether or not to purchase a pet? I'll admit that my track record with wisdom has suffered over the years. And every time a wrong choice is made (the puppy who lasted just five days comes to mind), one of two situations is happening: One, I haven't prayed for God's guidance. Or two, I feel the Holy Spirit's nudging but ignore it completely. Can you relate?

God's promise of wisdom is real and powerful and unbelievably unbelievable! Think about this: The Lord knows you better than you know yourself; he sees the intentions of those around you, and he designs a future that's best for you. Frankly, only a fool would throw away the promise that Isaiah 58:11 describes: "The Lord will guide you always; He will satisfy your needs in a sun-scorched land and will strengthen your frame. You will be like a well-watered garden, like a spring whose waters never fail."

In which areas of your life do *you* need God's wisdom? What decisions are on the horizon within the next few years? List some upcoming choices that could use a little guidance:

_____

_____

So how can you approach each day a wiser, more confident daughter of God? According to the Bible, it's first a matter of asking:

- "Show me your ways, O Lord, teach me your paths; guide me in your truth and teach me, for you are God my Savior, and my hope is in you all day long" (Psalm 25: 4–5).
- "If any of you lacks wisdom, he should ask God, who gives generously to all without finding fault, and it will be given to him" (James 1:5).

An interesting change happens when you ask God for wisdom: At the very moment you approach his throne for help, a shift occurs inside the heart. You begin to realize a desperate need for God. You understand that he, not you, knows what's best. And, sweet sister in Christ, the Father can work with a heart like that! When you acknowledge and respect him, then get ready for some answers! As Proverbs 9:10 says, "The reverence of the Lord is the beginning of wisdom."

When your heart is ready for God's guidance, he starts whispering those wise words. How will you hear them? It starts with a decision to dig in the Word. Let's practice getting wiser by studying Proverbs 4:5–13. Read the passage in your Bible, and then answer the questions below (Here's a hint for verses 6–9: The pronouns "she" and "her" refer to wisdom).

1. According to these verses, what steps should you take in order to receive wisdom?

_____

_____

2. What good things happen when you access God's wisdom?

_____

_____

3. What is the exact wording of verse thirteen?

_____

_____

I love this passage for many reasons, but I especially like the instruction about taking God's Word and holding it tight. Never, not even for one day, let it leave your heart. Make sure nothing silences it, not rebellion or distractions or laziness. This may be the biggest piece of advice I've heard in a while, straight from scripture: The wisdom of God is your life. Your life!

Daughter of God, are you tapping into the promise of wisdom? You can begin by praying, "Lord, I need your guidance. I am not wise, but I'm smart enough to know that your way is better. Show me what you want me to learn. I will search your Word, listen quietly, and obey the nudging of the Spirit."

Want to Dig Deeper?

Some people ignore the wisdom of the Lord, thus living foolishly. Read these verses to see how:

- Proverbs 14:9
- 1 Corinthians 2:14
- 1 Corinthians 3:18–19

_____

_____

_____

_____

Day Four: The Holy One Provides Strength

If you've known the Father for very long, you realize that clean living can zap your willpower! Yes, you're tucked safely under God's wings, protected and loved like never before. In addition, the Holy Spirit provides all the wisdom you need. The world, though, is just as sinful *after* you join the family—a fact that is frankly exhausting. So how does a Christian girl keep up her spiritual strength? By relying on his rock-solid promise:

> God is our refuge and strength, an ever present help in trouble. Therefore we will not fear, though the earth gives way and the mountains fall into the heart of the sea, though its waters roar and foam and the mountains quake with their surging.... The Lord Almighty is with us; the God of Jacob is our fortress.
>
> Psalm 46:1–3, 7

1. How often do you ask God for strength?

   _____

   _____

2. In what sorts of situations do you need God's strength?

   _____

   _____

3. What happens when you approach a situation without relying on the strength God provides?

   _____

   _____

Recently, I reflected on situations in my own life that need supernatural strength. Pretty soon, I realized that if God provides my needs—and he does—then the least I can do is give him glory. Whether he helps warriors win battles, prisoners endure suffering, or believers resist temptation, God's plan for his children is consistent: Do his will, access his power, and give him credit. And if you have a true heart for God, then your desire matches his exactly. Read these verses about the strength of God, and then write how these situations relate to your own life:

- "Who is God besides the Lord? Who is the rock except our God? It is God who arms me with strength and makes my way perfect. You [God] armed me with strength for battle; you made my enemies bow at my feet" (2 Samuel 22:32–33, 40).
- "God is faithful; He will not let you be tempted beyond what you can bear. But when you are tempted, he will also provide a way out so that you can stand up under it" (1 Corinthians 10:13).
- "If anyone speaks, he should do it as one speaking the very words of God. If anyone serves, he should do it with the strength God provides, so that in all things God may be praised through Jesus Christ" (1 Peter 4:11).

1. As 2 Samuel 22 shows, God's children face a continuous battle against the enemy. What battles against evil (Satan) do you fight in your day-to-day life?

_____

_____

2. In 1 Corinthians 10:13, God's strength is a way to resist temptation. Which temptations in your own life could use some strong resistance?

_____

_____

3. First Peter 4:11 explains the strength that's needed to speak up for God. List some opportunities in which his power can help you.

_____

_____

Over and over, God reminds us that living for him requires lots of spiritual muscle. And he's promised to bulk up the willing. So how does the process begin? Well, it's not a one-time steroid injection that instantly creates a super-Christian. Instead, building spiritual muscle is a gradual, steady commitment to wear "the armor of Christ." In your Bible, read

Ephesians 6:10–18. Then list the battle gear you'll need to access God's promise of strength:

1. Belt of _____   4. Shield of _____
2. Breastplate of _____   5. Helmet of _____
3. Feet of _____   6. Sword of the _____

Do you want God's strength? Do you need it? He's promised to go ahead of you into battle, and he's given you all the equipment you need. Thank him today for the almighty armor and the enduring promise of strength.

Want to Dig Deeper?

The very fact that God promises strength is proof that the world is hostile territory. If you're relying on him, however, it won't be long until you're actually thankful for the tough times. That's what Paul wrote in 2 Corinthians 12:10. Read the verse, and then explain what he means: "This is why, for Christ's sake, I delight in weaknesses, in insults, in hardships, in persecutions, in difficulties. For when I am weak, then I am strong."

1. How can Paul feel strong, even though he is faced with difficulties?

_____

_____

2. Explain Paul's last sentence.

_____

_____

3. When have you experienced Paul's thoughts during tough circumstances?

_____

_____

Day Five: The Holy One Reveals Answers

On the ride home from church, our family discussed all those prayers in which we ask for things. "Besides asking for salvation," I asked, "what's another prayer that God *always* answers in the way that we want?" The car fell silent as we thought about the requests we'd made, some answered with yes, some with no, and some with not yet.

Then, from the backseat full of kids, came a wise reply: "How about praying for God's will to be done? If you ask for what God wants, then the answer is always yes!" Amen, young one! Leaving it up to him means trusting that the outcome is always just right. Let's see what the Bible says about requests we make to God:

- "I waited patiently for the Lord; He turned to me and heard my cry. He lifted me out of the slimy pit, out of the mud and mire; He set my feet on a rock and gave me a firm place to stand.... I desire to do your will, O my God; your law is within my heart" (Psalm 40:1–2, 8).
- "[Jesus said], Our Father in heaven, hallowed be your name, your kingdom come, your will be done on earth as it is in heaven" (Matthew 6:9–10).

1. What did God do when the author of Psalm 40 brought his request to the Lord?

_____

_____

2. Whatever the outcome, why did the author of Psalm 40 desire God's will?

_____

_____

3. Besides Matthew 6:10, can you think of another instance when Jesus ended his prayer with "not my will, but yours"? (Hint: See Mark 14:32–41.)

_____

_____

God's promise to answer prayer appears throughout Scripture. My favorite verse about making requests is probably Psalm 37:4, which says, "Delight yourself in the Lord, and he will give you the desires of your heart." Did you pick up on the secret to rewarding prayer? When the heart is right—when the only intention is pleasing God—then he will give you everything you ask for! How do you think this works, exactly?

_____

_____

The daughter with a heart for God wants whatever brings him glory. She does not pray selfishly. And she realizes that regardless of the outcome, God knows best. Are you the kind of girl who's ready to say, "Not my way but his"? If so, then it's important to know the biblical way to pray. Read these passages, and then list the traits of a spirit-filled request:

- 2 Chronicles 7:14
- Proverbs 15:29

_____

_____

_____

There have been times when I wanted something from God, and I wanted it fast. Looking back, many of those prayers were immature and, frankly, not in my best interest. Over the years, though, I've seen with my own eyes that he takes good care of me. And so when my lips speak his name, I can honestly say, "Your will, Father," and mean it. How about you? What are some requests that weigh you down? Are you ready to surrender those burdens to God's timing? List several prayer requests, knowing that he promises a perfect solution to every concern:

_____

_____

Today, end your study time by talking with God about his desire for your life. Share with him your struggles, and then let the Father know that you trust him, whatever happens.

Want to Dig Deeper?

Sometimes, when the burden is especially difficult, prayers do not come easily. We may be too exhausted, hurt, or confused to say what we feel. Have no fear, though: When you are weary during troubled times, the Holy Spirit offers an energy boost. Read Romans 8:26–27, and write the promise for those with hurting hearts.

_____

_____

_____

_____

Week 4

Understanding What He Wants

During a recent Bible study, two students discussed why being a "good girl" is important. One said she wanted to make her parents proud. Another stated that college scholarships were based on character references. About that time, a twenty-something named Samantha added her two cents: "You'd better be good for the right reasons," she warned, "or pretty soon you'll find yourself on the rebellious side of the fence."

Samantha's comment—a wise one, I thought—made me think about my own views toward the good deeds God expects and the temptations that attract me. For example, do I deliberately run from disobedience, or do I try to justify it? Bottom line: Do I desire what God wants? Here's a personal question: Do *you*?

Before we daughters can help this hurting world, our own hearts must beat in rhythm with the Father's. To put it simply, we must love what God loves. We must want what God wants. And what he wants is an intimate relationship that's rooted in reverence and devotion. There's no other way to live, I've found. Have you discovered this truth for yourself?

> I know, my God, that you test the heart and are pleased with integrity. All these things have I given willingly and with honest intent. And now I have seen with joy how willingly your people who are here have given to you. O Lord, God of our Fathers Abraham, Isaac and Israel, keep this desire in the hearts of your people forever, and keep their hearts loyal to you.
>
> 1 Chronicles 29:17–18

Day One: The Lord Desires Your Reverence

For several weeks, we've studied the mind-blowing traits of God, along with the realization that he's unbelievably interested in us. More than interested, really. And once you personally understand his ferocious love—it's indescribable, isn't it?—then it clicks: You pursue him. You defend him. And, according to the Bible, you fear him. *Fear* him? Look at these verses:

- "Be sure to fear the Lord and serve him faithfully with all your heart; consider what great things he has done for you" (1 Samuel 12:24).
- "Let all the earth fear the Lord; let all people of the world revere him" (Psalm 33:8).
- "Charm is deceptive, and beauty is fleeting; but a woman who fears the Lord is to be praised" (Proverbs 31:30).

First things first: When the Bible refers to "fear of the Lord," there are two possible meanings. The first is trembling, scared-to-death fear that God's enemies knew well. You might remember that the Old Testament is full of bad guys running for their lives. This type of fear, borne out of disobedience, is *not* something God wants you to endure. He'd much rather spend his time enjoying another definition of fear, your reverence and awe. Review the verses listed in the previous paragraph, and think about these questions:

1. According to 1 Samuel 12:24, how can you revere God? Why should you fear him?

_____

_____

2. In Psalm 33:8, what word besides *fear* explains God's desire? What does this word mean to you?

_____

_____

3. Why should we praise a woman who fears the Lord, as Proverbs 31:30 states?

_____

_____

If your greatest desire is to please the one who loves you, then daily reverence is a must. For me, that means starting each morning on my knees (or sometimes on my face) as I approach the throne. What are some other ways you can show reverential fear?

_____

_____

A huge part of reverential fear, according to the Bible, is the desire to stay clean before him. Of course, the motive must center on one goal, to please the Lord (no obedience simply for the rewards, please. He can see right through that). Let's look at the connection between reverence and clean living:

1. Read Proverbs 3:7–8. How can you show reverence for God? What is the benefit when you do?

_____

_____

2. Read 2 Corinthians 7:1. Why should you keep your body and spirit clean? What are some ways that you can keep a clean body and spirit?

_____

_____

For years I've prayed, "Please, Lord, make me hate sin like you do. Make it turn my stomach, and make me run from it like the plague." Why do I pray this? One, it would be much easier to resist sin if the thought of it disgusted me. More than that, though, I want to honor my Father by clinging to goodness—to his desire for my awe and respect. Where is your heart when it comes to fear? Are you determined to show reverence by living cleanly?

Today try picturing the Lord on his throne. He's powerful but gentle, holy but approachable. Now imagine being beckoned to that throne. In your mind, do you bow before him in awe? Is your heart so full of reverence that you're about to burst? If so, then you're ready for the divine appointment. Yes, awestruck fear is what he desires, and, I'm sure you'll agree, it's what he deserves.

Want to Dig Deeper?

Reverence for God will be the main event in heaven. In your Bible, read the angels' song in Revelation 15:3–4. How could this verse apply for you personally?

_____

_____

_____

_____

Day Two: The Lord Desires Your Praise

One of my favorite times to praise God is during early morning walks in my neighborhood. For thirty minutes or so, my mouth is moving, my hands are animated, and my mental health is probably questioned as cars pass by. Well, if bragging on God is insane, then call me crazy! He is good. He is worthy. And he deserves our praise:

- "I call to the Lord, who is worthy of praise, and I am saved from my enemies" (2 Samuel 22:4).
- "Because your love is better than life, my lips will glorify you. I will praise you as long as I live, and in your name I will lift up my hands" (Psalm 63:3–4).

What exactly does it mean to praise God? Well, think of it as a time set aside to admire, acknowledge, or extol him. Basically, praising God means forgetting about yourself and focusing instead on worship. Let's give it a try:

1. What are some wonderful traits that describe God's character?

_____

_____

2. What are some wonderful ways that he shows his love?

_____

_____

3. What are some wonderful creations that you enjoy?

_____

_____

Think about the prayers of praise you've brought to the Father. Was it a pure offering of appreciation? Were you doing it out of routine? Or were you perhaps hoping to get something in return? Ouch. I admit that my praises have required some retooling, especially in terms of "buttering him up" for a request. How horrible that sounds! Sisters of mine, there is a difference between flattery and praise: Flattery builds up someone—in this case, God—in order to manipulate his actions. Praise, on the other hand, shows admiration just because you notice his awesomeness and want to give proper credit. There's no hidden agenda; you just can't help gushing about the greatness!

Isn't it humbling that Almighty God desires praise from your human lips? Think about it: He enjoys the continuous praise of angels and saints who are at his side. We're talking full-orchestra, spectacular adoration. And yet, he wants to hear it from you too. In your Bible, read what God desires from you:

1. In Psalm 96:1–4, how do believers praise the Father?

_____

_____

2. In Hebrews 13:15–16, how do believers praise the Father?

_____

_____

As these verses show, there are other ways to express praise besides prayer. When I'm exhausted and just need to think about his strength, that's praise. Often, a worship song gets stuck in my head and provides a praiseworthy soundtrack all day long. What are ways you admire or simply think about the awesomeness of God?

_____

_____

Yes, the Lord deserves our praise. Yes, he desires it. Here's an interesting thought about genuine praise, though: Perhaps *we* benefit more from praising God than *he* does! Could it be? Circle all the ways your heart is changed because of praise to the Father:

I am closer to God.
I am less critical.
I am less distracted.
I am less selfish.
I am more content.
I am more grateful.

In the past few years, God has taught me that praising him changes who I am. The more I adore him, the more I notice him. The more I notice him, the more I share him. And the more I share him, the more people meet him. That's cause for praise, right? Praise God! Praise God! Praise God!

Want to Dig Deeper?

As believers, we desperately want to become more like the Father every day; we desire to love like he loves and forgive like he forgives. When it comes to wanting praise for ourselves, however, we should seek the opposite. Read 1 Peter 5:5–6 in your Bible. What is it that God desires but we should not? Why do you think he tells us this?

_____

_____

_____

_____

Day Three: The Lord Desires Your Gratitude

When I was sixteen, my youth pastor explained the different kinds of prayer. He encouraged me to spend time praising, confessing, giving thanks, and interceding (praying for others). And while I tried my best to keep each category separate, the thanksgiving prayers kept creeping into my praises! Many years later, I still lump the two together. After all, it's impossible to acknowledge the works of God without immediately offering gratitude. And both—each separate but equal—are important to the Father:

- "Let us come before him with thanksgiving and extol him with music and song" (Psalm 95:2).
- "Enter his gates with thanksgiving and his courts with praise; give thanks to him and praise his name" (Psalm 100:4).

1. As you learned in Day Two, praising God means admiring him. How is thanksgiving different from praise?

_____

_____

2. Why do you think God desires your prayers of gratitude?

_____

_____

Most of us realize the importance of showing gratitude to God. We thank him for answered prayers, good health, and special friends. But how thankful are we when life gets messy? Is it possible to walk down a difficult road and offer sincere appreciation?

One example of gratitude during hard times is the Apostle Paul's outlook. As he wrote a letter to his friend Timothy, Paul was cruelly chained to the walls of a cold, dark dungeon. His health was failing, and he was lonely. Yet even with the odds stacked against him, Paul wrote, "I thank God, whom I serve as my forefathers did, with a clear conscience, as night and day I constantly remember you in my prayers" (2 Timothy 1:3). Put yourself in Paul's situation: How would you react to confinement, sickness, and loneliness?

_____ I'd be convinced that God was ignoring me.
_____ I'd be convinced that God was punishing me.
_____ I'd be convinced that prayer was useless.
_____ I'd be too angry to pray.
_____ I'd be too depressed to pray.
_____ I'd be too thankful *not* to pray.

Look at Paul's statement in 2 Timothy one more time. Even while suffering in prison, the gratitude was evident. Circle all the blessings that Paul acknowledged:

> Clear conscience
> Complete healing
> Friendship with believers
> God, the one he served
> Heritage of faith
> Quick rescue

Nowhere in the letter to Timothy did Paul ignore gratitude because of terrible circumstances. In fact, bad news didn't affect Paul's thanksgiving in the least! In your Bible, read 1 Thessalonians 5:16–18, another letter written by Paul. What did he say we should do when times are tough?

_____

_____

Are you able to give thanks when everything goes south? For the past year, I've thought about my own attitude of gratitude. Like Paul, I'm determined to focus on the gift that matters: eternal hope through Christ. And if that's all I ever receive from my Lord, then isn't that enough? After all, any other blessing that might (or might not) come my way is insignificant. In Hebrews 12:28–29, the author's words have become my own daily prayer of thanks. I encourage you to make it your prayer too: "Since we are receiving a kingdom that cannot be shaken, let us be thankful, and so worship God acceptably with reverence and awe, for our God is a consuming fire."

Want to Dig Deeper?

Some believe that every circumstance—heartache included—happens by God's design. ("The drunk-driving accident must have been God's will.") That's simply not true. Sin causes consequences that the Father never wanted for anyone. Read these verses that describe the troubles of those who deliberately disobey:

- Galatians 6:7–8
- Philippians 3:18–19

_____

_____

_____

_____

Day Four: The Father Desires Your Obedience

The thought of following rules makes some people a little nuts. They want complete control, and submitting to authority goes against the grain. Others, however, are happy to receive guidelines from parents, teachers, or employers. In which category do you fall—kicking-and-screaming rebellious or calm-and-collected obedient?

When it comes to believers, you'd assume that God's daughters *want* to obey his instructions. In theory, they cling to the wisdom, benefits, and necessity of submitting. Many times, though, the privilege of *want to* looks a lot like the dreaded *have to*. Below, circle all the reasons you obey God:

Enjoy a clean conscience
Fear his punishment
Hope to be an influence
Love the Lord
Need his guidance
Want rewards

If you marked any less than desirable answers, thanks for your honesty. Over and over, I see young women making the right choice out of obligation to church, parents, or to their own ideas. And while it's never a *bad* thing to obey God's teachings, the right motive is a big, big deal. Look at these passages about the one acceptable reason for obedience:

- "Jesus replied, 'If anyone loves me, he will obey my teaching. My Father will love him, and we will come to him and make our home with him. He who does not love me will not obey my teaching'" (John 14:23–24).
- "This is love for God: to obey his commands. And his commands are not burdensome, for everyone born of God overcomes the world" (1 John 5:3–4).

1. What should be the primary reason you choose to obey God?

_____

_____

2. According to Jesus, what does disobedience say about your relationship with him?

_____

_____

3. If you love God, then his commands are not burdensome. What does this mean?

_____

_____

Let's be clear: Although we honor God through obedience, Christianity is not about perfectly following the rules. If this were the case, then all of us would be in trouble! Thankfully, Jesus wiped away the to-do list and replaced it with his perfect sacrifice. No, we are not required to master every command to be his child. But we _want_ to. We love him. And more than anything, we want to please the one who loved us first.

Obedience is much easier, I think, when we trust the one in charge. Aren't you more inclined to follow someone who's experienced, wise, and caring? And doesn't joyful obedience increase when we love the one in authority? If so, then you understand why obedience to God—who fits all these attributes—makes a lot of sense.

One of my favorite passages describes obedience without question. He speaks, and we happily adjust to his voice. Sounds easy, huh? Just listen and follow. Read John 10:27.

1. Jesus _____ us, so he knows what's best for us.

2. In order to follow Jesus's teachings, we have to
_____ him.

The key to joyful obedience, I believe, is a healthy relationship with the Father. This means knowing him intimately through prayer, Bible study, and discussions with mature believers. Before long, you'll love him deeply, and following him will be a privilege. Today, why not ask God to place within you a fresh desire to obey his word?

Want to Dig Deeper?

Think about this: Even Jesus Christ, the perfect one, knew the importance of obedience to his Father. Read these verses, and then write your thoughts:

- "[Jesus said] If you obey my commands, you will remain in my love, just as I have obeyed my Father's commands and remain in his love" (John 15:10).
- "And being found in appearance as a man, he humbled himself and became obedient to death—even death on a cross!" (Philippians 2:8).
- "Although he was a son, he learned obedience from what he suffered and, once made perfect, he became the source of eternal salvation for all who obey him ..." (Hebrews 5:8–9).

_____

_____

_____

_____

Day Five: The Lord Desires Your Loyalty

When it comes to personal relationships with friends or family, how important is the trait of loyalty? I think we all want someone's complete devotion. Who in your own life is loyal to you? List their names here:

_____

_____

Just as you need the loyalty of loved ones, God desires the same devotion from you, his child. My prayer is that your commitment would be constant, visible, and wholehearted. When this happens—a fierce loyalty rooted so deeply that nothing could turn you from him—the blessings flow.

In the Bible, Job loved God with all his heart, even when disaster struck. His friends offered all kinds of advice, some good and some bad, but Job's loyalty to the Father never wavered. The following passage, while spoken by one of his accusing friends, nevertheless offers beautiful truth about loyalty's reward:

> If you devote your heart to him and stretch out your hands to him, if you put away the sin that is in your hand and allow no evil to dwell in your tent, then you will lift up your face without shame; you will stand firm and without fear. You will surely forget your trouble, recalling it only as waters gone by. Life will be brighter than noonday, and darkness will become like morning. You will be secure because there is hope; you will look about you and take your rest in safety.
>
> Job 11:13–18

1. According to the passage, what are several ways you can show loyalty to God?

_____

_____

2. What are several blessings that come along when you are devoted to the Lord?

_____

_____

3. What part of the passage is especially meaningful to you?

_____

_____

When God asks for total commitment, he's clear about wanting all of you forever: no divided loyalties; God only, for always. No putting it off; God only, right now. In your Bible, read these verses about his idea of sincere devotion:

1. In 1 Chronicles 28:9, what does God desire?

_____

_____

2. In Ezekiel 33:31, what does God *not* desire?

_____

_____

Like many believers, my loyalty to God has suffered from disobedience, selfishness, and downright stupidity. For a short period, Paul's warning in 2 Corinthians 11:3 described me to a T: "I am afraid that just as Eve was deceived by the serpent's tricks, your minds may somehow be led astray from your sincere and pure devotion to Christ." I was led astray all right, tricked into sins that compromised my loyalties. Before I knew it, my walk with God had detoured from sincere devotion to hypocritical rebellion. Do I regret it? You bet. There are always consequences when sin enters the picture, and although I'm completely forgiven, it saddens me still to know that I broke my Father's heart.

If you have denied God the devotion he desires, then the first step is genuine repentance. He will indeed forgive and forget. Know, though, that in this new day, the key to continued loyalty is a consistent relationship with the Father. In the book of Jude, verses 20–21 explain how to do it: "Dear friends, build yourselves up in your most holy faith and pray in the Holy Spirit. Keep yourselves in God's love as you wait for the mercy of our Lord Jesus Christ to bring you to eternal life." Amen!

Want to Dig Deeper?

In order to show God your loyalty, it's important to turn away from what he despises. In your Bible, look at these verses to see what should appear on your not-gonna-do list:

- Proverbs 6:16–19
- 1 John 2:9

_____

_____

_____

_____

Week 5

Acknowledging What He Conquers

If Christianity had its own cheering squad, then my student Brianna would be the hands-down captain. She's enthusiastic, encouraging, and convincing. Whenever she shares God with classmates, it's an energetic chant of awesome benefits: joy, peace, and purpose. What a great promoter for Team God! And while her delivery may focus only on the blessings, I'll say this for a young woman who loves her Father: After listening to Brianna's passion, everyone within hearing distance is cheering too!

Hopefully, though, both Brianna and the rest of her squad realize that bad things still happen to blessed people. We get sick, disappointed, and criticized, just like those who don't know the Lord. But here's the gigantic difference: We can find the good in the middle of each crisis. Contentment and protection? All there, guarding us against discouragement and harm. Yep, Christians tackle this old world with more safety equipment than a football team!

This week we'll see how the Father provides real victory during the ickiest days. He alone is your most valuable player. You're on the winning team, my sister, a truth that makes even the heaviest hearts do cartwheels!

> I know what it is to be in need, and I know what it is to have plenty. I have learned the secret of being content in any and every situation, whether well fed or hungry, whether living in plenty or in want. I can do everything through him who gives me strength.
>
> Philippians 4:12–13

Day One: The Father Overcomes Confusion

If there's one thing I know for sure, it's that Satan *hates* a clear-headed Christian. You see, if he can make you second guess your motives, abilities, and beliefs, then the rest is a piece of cake. Pretty soon, his scheme will snowball into all kinds of confusing thoughts. So don't fall for the tricks, sweet daughter of God. After all, Satan is "a liar and the father of lies," according to John 8:44. Instead, trust the one who provides order and peace, as 1 Corinthians 14:33 reminds us.

Sadly, it's easy to fall into the trap of confusion. We receive all kinds of conflicting advice, and sometimes it's difficult to get it right. Place a check by the scenarios that threaten clear thinking:

____ Choosing the right _____. (Fill in the blank with whatever comes to mind.)
____ Deciding how or when to talk with someone about God.
____ Detecting which people around me are trustworthy.
____ Understanding the mysteries of my faith.
____ Trusting God's goodness when I see so much evil.

So how can we kick Satan's confusion to the curb and embrace the confidence of God instead? Well, first we must realize that *un*certainty is *un*necessary. Look at these verses about God's promise to cut a clear path:

- "You are my lamp, O Lord; the Lord turns my darkness into light. With your help I can advance against a troop; with my God I can scale a wall" (2 Samuel 22:29–30).
- "[God says] I will lead the blind by ways they have not known, along unfamiliar paths I will guide them; I will turn the darkness into light before them and make the rough places smooth. These are the things I will do; I will not forsake them" (Isaiah 42:16).

Regardless of what those fears whisper in your ear, here is the truth, straight from the lips of God: "I will lead the blind." And he will, every time! If you're having trouble letting this clear-cut promise sink in, then think about some truths I've learned over the years:

1. Just because something is unclear to you doesn't mean that it's unclear to God. If you're following him every day, then you won't make a wrong step because he won't let you.
2. If you don't understand something at the moment, that's okay. Trusting the one who knows it all keeps your mind clear and ready for the next step.

The Bible gives us practical tips for keeping confusion at arm's length. In your Bible, find the following verses to see God's strategy for your healthy state of mind:

1. James 3:13–17

   • Which traits pave the way for wisdom?
   • Which traits give way to Satan's confusion?

_____

_____

2. 1 John 5:14

   • How should you approach God?
   • What should you do when you need answers?

_____

_____

3. Proverbs 4:25–26

   • Where should you look when confusion is around?
   • What's the key to success (being established)?

_____

_____

Are you ready to reject Satan's confusion? Then replace your mind and heart with the promises of the Father. He will give you clarity, peace, and direction for every decision. It's as easy as asking!

Want to Dig Deeper?

When we feel confused, the Bible tells us to start with the basics: pray, trust, and obey. That way, our hearts will be ready when the answers come. Read Ephesians 5:15–21, and then list the pleasing actions of a clear-headed believer:

_____

_____

_____

_____

Day Two: The Father Stamps Out Loneliness

For me, there's nothing worse than feeling lonely. Whether I'm at a crowded party or by myself at home, the isolation is sometimes depressing. Have you ever sensed that you were alone in your beliefs? At times, I've felt like an outcast, the one voice in the room who is passionate about God. Apparently, it's a common scenario, since King David also pleaded to the Father, "Turn to me and be gracious to me, for I am lonely and afflicted" (Psalm 25:16). How about you? When has your devotion to God resulted in a solo act?

_____

_____

Whatever your experience, God knows all about it. In fact, he recognized Adam's loneliness right away, saying that it was "not good for man to be alone" (Genesis 2:18). And his Son Jesus experienced the pain of isolation firsthand:

- "Jesus replied, 'Foxes have holes and birds of the air have nests, but the Son of Man has no place to lay his head'" (Luke 9:58).
- "The Son of Man in his day will be like the lightning, which flashes and lights up the sky from one end to the other. But first he must suffer many things and be rejected by this generation" (Luke 17:24–25).

Several truths in these verses jump out at me. One, I don't need a lot of friends or things to be content. Two, the loneliness I might experience is always worth it in the long run. And three, my sad little pity party is nothing compared to what Jesus suffered!

No matter how lonely you feel, always remember that you travel with a continuous party of heavenly hosts. (And this particular group is better than any human crowd I know of!) For starters, the Holy Spirit encourages, empowering you from the inside. The Son understands what you're up against. And the Father, without hesitation, wraps those loving arms around you. Read these verses about God's promise to keep you company:

- "The Lord himself goes before you and will be with you; he will never leave you nor forsake you. Do not be afraid; do not be discouraged" (Deuteronomy 31:8).
- "'Though the mountains be shaken and the hills be removed, yet my unfailing love for you will not be shaken nor my covenant of peace be removed,' says the Lord, who has compassion on you" (Isaiah 54:10).

1. When you feel lonely, how can these verses bring comfort and encouragement?

_____

_____

2. When do you need reminding of God's unfailing love?

_____

_____

When I've found myself standing alone, God has given me courage. More often than not, he has also provided a like-minded friend to stand alongside me. And believe me, two Christians joined together are powerful. Read these verses about strength in small numbers, and then write the advantages of a tight-knit, believing minority:

1. Proverbs 27:17

_____

_____

2. Ecclesiastes 4:10–12

_____

_____

3. Hebrews 10:24–25

_____

_____

Are you so in love with God that the cost of following him—the threat of isolation—is no big deal? Read these words by the Apostle Paul, thinking about your own commitment, whatever the cost:

> At my first defense, no one came to my support, but everyone deserted me. May it not be held against them. But the Lord stood at my side and gave me strength, so that through me the message might be fully proclaimed and all the Gentiles might hear it. And I was delivered from the lion's mouth.
> 2 Timothy 4:16–17

Want to Dig Deeper?

Even though most of us prefer a crowd over a table for one, there are times that being alone is best. Read these verses, listing some advantages of the occasional timeout:

- Exodus 23:1–2
- Matthew 14:23
- 2 Corinthians 6:17–18

_____

_____

_____

_____

Day Three: The Father Eases Exhaustion

More than any other lesson, today's topic relates to me. Not long ago, the stress of daily life overwhelmed and discouraged me. To be honest, I didn't know how to get off the merry-go-round. And while the items on my to-do list were important, in the long run they weren't good for my body or spirit. Then it occurred to me: How could sleepless nights and crazy schedules be God's plan? Had I ever asked my Father about the overwhelming commitments? Then there were the things I *had* to accomplish, like school and work and laundry. The thought, even now, is exhausting!

I'm wondering if your life resembles my battle with fatigue. What prevents you from resting in the way that God intends? Make a list of must-do responsibilities in your everyday life. Then write any extra activities that take up your time:

1. Day-to-day "must do" responsibilities

_____

_____

2. Day-to-day "optional" activities

_____

_____

Knowing how to rest is the Father's specialty. Look at these verses about God's commitment to help his tired and worn-out children:

- "My soul finds rest in God alone; my salvation comes from him. He alone is my rock and my salvation; He is my fortress; I will never be shaken" (Psalm 62:1–2).
- "Even youths grow tired and weary, and young men stumble and fall; but those who hope in the Lord will renew their strength. They will soar on wings like eagles; they will run and not grow weary, they will walk and not be faint" (Isaiah 40:30–31).

After reading these promises, we can learn a few truths about exhaustion: One, it happens to the most obedient of believers. Two, it should be temporary. And three, with God's help, we can find the rest we need.

Thankfully, the Bible shows us how to combine work with rest. There *is* a balance, you know. Read these verses, and then reflect on God's plan for work and rest:

- "By the seventh day God had finished the work he had been doing; so on the seventh day he rested from all his work. And God blessed the seventh day and made it holy, because on it he rested from all the work of creating that he had done" (Genesis 2:2–3).
- "When Moses's hands grew tired, they took a stone and put it under him and he sat on it. Aaron and Hur held his hands up—one on one side, one on the other—so that his hands remained steady till sunset" (Exodus 17:12).
- "Unless the Lord builds the house, its builders labor in vain. Unless the Lord watches over the city, the watchmen stand guard in vain" (Psalm 127:1).

1. In Genesis 2:2–3, why do you think God provided the example of rest? In your own life, do you use spare moments to add more activities?

_____

_____

2. In Exodus 17:12, what did Moses learn about leaning on someone when the job was difficult? In your own life, how can others help you with the must-do-today list?

_____

_____

3. In Psalm 127:1, what do we learn about commitments the Lord never asked us to make? In your own life, are there things—good things, even—that need to go?

_____

_____

Today's world spins at an exhausting pace, but I hopped off the ride with a desperate prayer: "Father, I am weary. Show me what is necessary, and help me see what is not." Then I studied my calendar, asking God to reveal activities to eliminate—at least for the time being. Three commitments—two of them church related—leapt off the page. Now, a year later, God has helped me simplify and focus. He's shown me how to rest, eat well, and have fun. And there's plenty of time (go figure!) for the necessities: Sharing Christ, loving family, and even doing laundry! Yes, there's plenty of time for abundant life when we follow *his* timetable.

How about you? Are you ready to jump from draining exhaustion to energized fulfillment? Talk with God today about the work *and* the rest that he's planned. It'll do wonders for your spirit. And your busy, busy calendar.

Want to Dig Deeper?

While on earth, Jesus set an example of rest for us to follow. Read these verses that record his plan for being rested and ready:

- John 4:1–8
- Luke 5:15–16
- Mark 1:35

1. In John 4:1–8, what are Jesus's physical needs? How can you address your physical needs in the fight against exhaustion?

_____

_____

2. In Luke 5:15–16, how does Jesus quiet his spirit? What are some situations in which you could use this strategy?

_____

_____

3. In Mark 1:35, when does Jesus spend time with his father? How can you be fresh and ready for God?

_____

_____

Day Four: The Father Soothes Disappointment

Here you are, a young woman who's strengthened her father-daughter relationship for five weeks now. If you've made it this far, then I'm assuming your love for God is genuine and deepening. You're maturing into someone who knows that "his divine power has given us everything we need for life and godliness through our knowledge of him who called us by his own glory and goodness" (2 Peter 1:3). Yes, through God alone, you have everything you need.

What you *want*, though, may be a different story. Oh, how I hate disappointment, especially when my wish list is ever growing! Are you thinking of some recent disappointments in your own life? Circle any of these that apply:

> Unanswered questions
> Unexpected change of plans
> Unfair treatment
> Unrealistic goals
> Unreliable people
> Unsupportive friends or family

These kinds of situations—the ones when daughters feel dejected— are the times when faith is all you have. You must believe in his love for you. And you must trust that he knows best. Read these words to see how God conquers distress:

- "Be strong and take heart, all you who hope in the Lord" (Psalm 31:24).
- "And we know that in all things God works for the good of those who love him, who have been called according to his purpose" (Romans 8:28).

Judging from the tone of these verses, believers have always suffered disappointment. But they've also overcome sadness, courtesy of a faithful God. Let me share with you, from experience, the peace of knowing it'll be okay. Whatever "it" happens to be, you can believe that he is aware of the situation and is also in charge of it. (Don't you just *love* him?)

I used to assume that believers—the ones who, like me, followed God closely—were usually content. And in lots of ways this was true: Hard work brought success, and wholesome reputations ensured respect. So imagine my surprise when disappointment plopped down in my life and stayed awhile. One bad thing after another helped me see that sadness visits everyone. Healing came eventually, and one reason was my daily fix of Romans 5:1–5. In your Bible, study these verses carefully before responding to the following questions:

1. During times of suffering, what should believers do?

_____

_____

2. What three qualities are strengthened during disappointing times?

_____

_____

3. Why are we daughters of God not disappointed?

_____

_____

If we trust him, precious daughters, then we won't be disappointed in the outcome. Recently, a missionary facing cancer offered some advice. Instead of questioning the sad event, he explained, why not roll up your sleeves and ask, "What now, Lord? How do you want me to handle this terrible situation?" What an attitude of trust! Of action! Of obedience! Are you up to it? Oh, I hope so!

Some empty fish nets in John 21 tell a similar story. How disappointed Peter must have been, fishing all night with no success. Then Jesus showed up with some instructions, Peter rolled up his sleeves, and pretty soon he was hauling in full nets, exclaiming, "It is the Lord!" (John 21:7). Will you listen for the Father's wisdom when disappointment strikes? If so, then hope will appear, and soon you'll be echoing Peter's words of praise: "It is the Lord! It is the Lord!"

Want to Dig Deeper?

Psalm 31 describes David's frustration as King Saul is on the prowl. Read the entire chapter, and then record some details of David's reactions as the drama unfolds.

1. David's cry for help (verses 1–8)

_____

_____

2. David's stressful situation (verses 9–13)

_____

_____

3. David's hope in the Lord (verses 14–24)

_____

_____

Day Five: The Father Conquers Doubt

Do you tend to question everything? Or do you usually accept whatever you're told? Everybody, at one time or other, doubts something. It's just human nature, I guess, to wonder what's right or real. For those with hearts for God, though, some truths are crystal clear: We know he is there, we know he cares, and we know he has a plan. How can we be so sure? Circle the reasons that are especially true for you:

> I'm amazed at the historical growth of Christianity.
> I'm awed by the miracle of nature.
> I've experienced God's real, intimate presence.
> I've felt the Holy Spirit speak to me through Scripture and prayer.
> I've seen the power of prayer, and I trust in God's promise to provide.

For daughters who barely know God, it's easy to see why they'd eventually doubt. Shallow roots have nothing to cling to, but those with deep, abiding intimacy are convinced he exists, he loves, and he reigns. When did you first get to know him? And when have you seen him work, without a doubt, in your own life?

_____

_____

While I never question the existence of God, there are times when I have doubted my ability to serve him. After all, I'm such a mess-up sometimes! Do you feel the same? If so, then it's important to remember who generates these thoughts. They are *not* from your heavenly Father. Instead, they are lies from the evil one, insecurities to downplay God's power through you. Read this passage about the author of doubt, along with the reassuring truth:

> We know that we are children of God and that the whole world is under the control of the evil one. We know also that the Son of God has come and has given us understanding, so that we may know him who is true. And we are in him who is true—even in his Son Jesus Christ. He is the true God and eternal life.
>
> 1 John 5:19–20

1. We believers are not of this world. Why does this bring relief?

_____

_____

2. We are children of God. In this passage, what truths do we know for sure?

_____

_____

3. What does the Son of God give us instead of doubt?

_____

_____

What good news! As daughters of God, we don't have to doubt our good standing with the Lord. No, we can't please him on our own, but we don't have to. Christ provided the way for acceptance without judgment. It's a beautiful, freeing truth: We can be confident that our devotion to God, even if it's not perfect, is enough. In your Bible, read Matthew 14:22–33, the story of a disciple who experienced both doubt and understanding.

1. Why do you think Peter had enough confidence to get out of the boat?

_____

_____

2. At what point did he doubt the miracle?

_____

_____

3. Do your own doubts surface when storms arise? According to verses 29–31, what's the secret to renewed confidence?

_____

_____

Like Peter, we must learn to trust, no matter what the world claims. The key, as always, is staying close to the one who erases doubt. He, the Father, stands ready to assure, equip, and reward: "So do not throw away your confidence; it will be richly rewarded. You need to persevere so that when you have done the will of God, you will receive what he has promised" (Hebrews 10:35–36).

Want to Dig Deeper?

Early believers, like us, were imperfect. Sometimes they trusted, and other days the doubts rolled like thunder. Read the accounts of two followers who reacted differently to the promises of God:

1. Abraham (Romans 4:18–21)
2. Thomas (John 20:24–29)
3. Which follower's reaction more closely resembles your own personality? How can you develop a faith that is strong and consistent, even when the odds are stacked against you?

_____

_____

_____

_____

Week 6

Believing What He Says

When people meet Maria for the first time, she seems very sweet and quiet. A great listener, she is perfectly content letting others get all the attention. In fact, sometimes during Bible study I have to "shush" everyone else so that Maria can contribute. Not that she minds at all. Her kind, peaceful spirit is one reason she has so many friends.

One night, though, Maria walked into Bible study with a fire in her belly. She had come alive! A biology teacher had stated, in front of the entire class, that her answer to an evolution question was "ridiculous." He went on to criticize her beliefs, calling them "ignorant and improbable." My heart broke for Maria, picturing her tortured face as the teacher lectured her. But as she told the story, Maria didn't seem embarrassed. Instead, she was ready to fight for the God she loved! "Pray about my next step," she told each of us. "I know this battle will be difficult, but I must defend my Father. He has promised to give me strength, and I believe him." Go, Maria!

If your relationship with God is going to flourish, then those action verbs must kick in. You must not only believe the promises, but you must also put them into play. Boldly *tell* him what you need. Bravely *defend* him when it's time. Faithfully *trust* him with your life. And most of all, fiercely *love* him with your heart. That's what separates a distant daughter from a devoted one. I'm believing, sweet sister, that you're the latter.

> In that day they will say, "Surely this is our God; we trusted in him, and he saved us. This is the Lord; we trusted in him; let us rejoice and be glad in his salvation."
>
> Isaiah 25:9

Day One: Trust Him with Your Life

Let me confess that the title of this lesson needs a little tweaking. Obviously, trusting God is important. And with him in control, your life is in excellent hands. While a statement like this looks good on paper, though, how trusting are you on the day-to-day path? You know, the one that reveals just a glimmer of light on a winding road? That's harder, huh? But trust, according to God, is a daily decision to take one step, knowing that he'll light the whole path when it's time. So let's change the title a bit, making it crystal clear: Trust him with your *daily* life. Several passages remind us that God lights the way for full-blown trust:

- "For you have delivered me from death and my feet from stumbling, that I may walk before God in the light of life" (Psalm 56:13).
- "When Jesus spoke again to the people, he said, 'I am the light of the world. Whoever follows me will never walk in darkness, but will have the light of life'" (John 8:12).
- "You are a chosen people, a royal priesthood, a holy nation, a people belonging to God, that you may declare the praises of him who called you out of darkness and into his wonderful light" (1 Peter 2:9).

1. I walk before God in the light of _____.

2. Believers who follow Jesus will _____ walk in darkness.

3. Followers of God have been taken out of _____ and into wonderful _____.

As a teen, I struggled with trusting God to lead me one step at a time. In fact, I wasn't comfortable with this setup at all. Maybe it's typical for most seventeen-year-olds, but I wanted to know several things pronto: the college I'd attend, the career I'd find, and the man I'd marry. Does this desire to peek into a crystal ball sound familiar? What part of God's plan would you like to see right now?

_____

_____

Sure, we're curious to know the future, whether it's ten years from now or ten minutes. But really, if we know it all, then what's the point of trust? That's why our heavenly Father, for the most part, reveals one step at a time. Can you think of some benefits to *not* seeing the entire picture? Place a check by the statements that cross your mind:

_____1. I learn to rely on God daily.

_____2. I handle stress better when I don't feel it all at once.

_____3. I live with excited anticipation of what God will do.

_____4. I surrender my selfishness to God's plan.

_____5. I influence people who watch me live by faith.

If you have a heart for God, then you're okay with his plan. You trust him with your day and with your life. Let's be completely transparent for a minute: Is it tough for you to believe that he'll come through? As a seasoned follower, let me offer some advice: Don't obsess over the details you cannot see. That's where trouble lies, since believers who get ahead of God often get off track. They force circumstances into divine "signs" or ignore anything that doesn't fit their idea of the "big picture." Most of all, daughters who worry about their long-term futures lose sight of daily dependence. And daily (sometimes hourly) dependence is right where he wants you.

Even if you don't know what the end of the road holds, God clearly points the way to today's agenda. What do these verses say about following him right now?

- 1 Samuel 12:14
- Matthew 16:24

_____

_____

How do you feel about trusting him with today's agenda? Are you willing? If so, then that's all you need to do. Just seek him daily, and pretty soon that trusting heart of yours will mature into unwavering faith. You'll rest confidently because the one who sees it all guides every precious step.

Want to Dig Deeper?

Sometimes people worry about their futures because they can't control what happens. In Matthew 6:25–34, Jesus had some wise and comforting words for those who stress about tomorrow. Read this passage as a reminder that God will take good care of you. What words do you find especially comforting?

_____

_____

_____

_____

Day Two: Tell Him What You Need

From the time I learned to talk, my parents encouraged me to tell God everything, and I mean *everything*. A misplaced homework assignment? Ask God where it is. Nervous about a swim meet? Tell God about it. My heavenly Father listened patiently to the curly-haired kid ramble on and on. And thankfully, I learned quickly that when he is included, everything seems better. If you're a longtime prayer warrior like me, then you know the truth of these verses:

- "Cast your care on the Lord and he will sustain you; He will never let the righteous fall" (Psalm 55:22).
- "Therefore I tell you, whatever you ask for in prayer, believe that you have received it, and it will be yours" (Mark 11:24).
- "Is any one of you in trouble? He should pray" (James 5:13).

I don't think any of us would argue against the power of prayer. Scripture is full of believers who sought God and heard from him. And now, in the twenty-first century, he is still in the business of listening to his children. You have probably poured your heart out to God on at least one occasion. If you feel comfortable, briefly describe the reason for your prayer:

_____

_____

Even though God is ready and waiting to talk, not everyone pursues a praying lifestyle. Have you ever known someone who hardly ever prayed? Or someone who never prayed for herself but asked others to intercede for her? I am surprised by the number of believers—daughters of God—who don't take advantage of the earth-to-heaven communication plan. One woman I know often comes to me with prayer requests, admitting that she is uncomfortable talking with God on her own. What are some reasons that believers might find it awkward to pray?

_____

_____

Maybe it's guilt. Or maybe it's insecurity. Who knows why children of God avoid talking with their creator? Regardless, the Bible assures us that God is all ears, ready and willing to chat with his kids. In fact, the thing he loves most is to fellowship with us. In your Bible, read these verses to see his kind, loving response to our prayers:

1. In 2 Chronicles 7:14, what will God do when his people humble themselves and pray?

_____

_____

2. According to Psalm 6:9, what does the Lord hear and accept?

_____

_____

3. What does Lamentations 3:22–23 say about God's compassion for his children?

_____

_____

More than anything, the Father desires a close, consistent relationship with his children, you included. And that means coming to him with every concern, no matter what. What are some situations that might prevent you from maintaining a healthy prayer life?

_____ avoiding a topic that may be unpleasant
_____ being too busy for an unrushed conversation
_____ rebelling and unwilling to change
_____ thinking that prayer won't make a difference
_____ viewing prayer as a dull routine

Daughters of God know that regular, sincere prayer is vital to holy intimacy. It is what he wants. It is what we need. First Thessalonians 5:16–18 is a wonderful passage about prayer, helping me remember the loving command to approach a Holy God: "Be joyful always; pray continually; give thanks in all circumstances, for this is God's will for you in Christ Jesus." Why not go before the throne now with your whole heart?

Want to Dig Deeper?

In the gospel of Luke, the disciples asked Jesus to teach them to pray. Read Luke 11:1–4 to pick up some valuable truths for approaching the Father. Then compare this passage with Jesus's warning about displeasing prayers found in Matthew 6:5–7. Are your conversations with God music to his ears? Write a short, sincere prayer to the Father, straight from a daughter's heart.

_____

_____

_____

_____

Day Three: Defend Him When It's Time

More than ever, defending your faith takes incredible strength, wisdom, and passion. When the world thinks you're nuts for trusting an invisible God, it's important to speak. When friends question your convictions, it's time to stick up for the Father. But sometimes, to be honest, standing tall takes guts when everyone else is sitting down. What are some biblical beliefs that are important to you but practically ignored by others?

When I was in high school, the cafeteria was a circus of crowded tables that signified social status. Athletes sat in a certain section, artsy kids in another, and so on. And then there was Teri, a perfectly nice girl who didn't fit any particular group, mainly due to her appearance. No one invited her to join them—ever. One day the Holy Spirit prompted me into action, and I asked Teri to join my group of classmates. She smiled gratefully, sat down, and then all my friends rolled their eyes and ignored her. The next day, they informed me that there wasn't room at the table for Teri. You guessed it: The time to stand had come. For the next few weeks, at a cozy table for two, Teri and I had some great conversations, and the Lord blessed both of us through that experience.

For girls in love with their God, defending the truth is a no-brainer. We faithfully obey, regardless of temporary discomfort. Look at this passage about gutsy commitment:

> So then, brothers, stand firm and hold to the teachings we passed on to you, whether by word of mouth or by letter. May our Lord Jesus Christ himself and God our Father, who loved us and by his grace gave us eternal encouragement and good hope, encourage your hearts and strengthen you in every good deed and word.
>
> 2 Thessalonians 2:15–17

1. What specific truths should we firmly uphold wherever we go?

---

2. Why is it important to surround ourselves with Christian mentors?

_____

_____

3. What qualities does God promise those who defend his truth?

_____

_____

Through the years, I've met young women who see the need to act but doubt their abilities to do so. Sounds a lot like Moses, doesn't it? If you'll recall, God told the tongue-tied shepherd to get ready for the stand of a lifetime: "So now, go. I am sending you to Pharaoh to bring my people the Israelites out of Egypt" (Exodus 3:10). Immediately, Moses began listing reasons why he was not qualified. Look at these verses, and list some of Moses's excuses:

- Exodus 3:11
- Exodus 4:1
- Exodus 4:10

_____

_____

_____

I'm honestly puzzled about Moses seeing a burning bush, hearing a booming voice, and yet questioning God's ability to choose the right man. Even after several miracles right before his eyes—a stick turning into a snake, for one—Moses still begged, "Oh Lord, please send someone else to do it" (Exodus 4:13). But before we're too hard on Moses, let's get personal: How many times have we withdrawn when we needed to step up? Do we look for someone else to defend God's truth?

Today's world needs a young woman or two to defend the Father. His voice is being silenced through government, television, music, and literature. People you know have inaccurate beliefs about the one you love. Maybe it's time for you to tell them. Or show them. Or, at the very least, pray for them. What are some ways that you can defend the truth about your Father?

_____

_____

When you have the chance to stand, get excited! God is using you, equipping you, and blessing you. And if the task seems intimidating, take his words to heart: "Who gave man his mouth? Who makes him deaf or mute? Who gives him sight or makes him blind? Is it not I, the Lord? Now go; I will help you speak and will teach you what to say" (Exodus 4:11).

Want to Dig Deeper?

If you've ever taken a stand that seemed to go nowhere, don't be discouraged. Read 1 Corinthians 15:58, and then summarize Paul's encouragement for believers who defend the one they love.

_____

_____

_____

_____

Day Four: Claim Him When It's Difficult

We're almost at the end of our journey, a crash course in unwavering devotion. I pray that a newfound, deep appreciation for the Father has taken root. During the study, have you grown in your reverence? Your love? If you're like me, the more you know him, the more you're overwhelmed with his character. God is so *big* and yet so intimate. He's so *just* and yet so merciful. He's so *ancient* and yet so timely. He's so, well, unfathomable!

And he is on the throne, even when our worlds are crumbling. This is a tough concept, isn't it? All around us we see the devastating results of Satan's hand. The newspaper is often depressing, and many times daughters know terrible pain firsthand. What examples come to mind when you think of the evil in your own backyard?

Whatever you've written, I have no doubt that it's a sickening picture of a sinful world. And yet, despite sad and unimaginable horrors, Holy God still reigns. Hallelujah! Several verses in Psalms speak specifically about the Lord's triumph in the midst of Satan's ploys:

- "Do not fret because of evil men or be envious of those who do wrong; for like the grass they will soon wither, like green plants they will soon die away. Trust in the Lord and do good; dwell in the land and enjoy safe pasture" (Psalm 37:1–4).
- "Have mercy on me, O God, have mercy on me, for in you my soul takes refuge. I will take refuge in the shadow of your wings until the disaster has passed" (Psalm 57:1).

1. Which words or phrases in these passages are comforting to you?

---

2. When have you experienced God's presence in the midst of evil?

Many people struggle with unbelief when their faith is tested. For some, claiming God's presence in the midst of tragedy is especially difficult. Below, check all the reasons that people might fall away during challenging times:

____ They are unfamiliar with the Bible's promises.
____ They are too worried or exhausted to pray.
____ They don't know God in a personal way.
____ They fear that God's punishment is underway.
____ They have no past stories of faith to encourage them.

Unfortunately, nonbelievers aren't the only ones who suffer from scenarios like these. I've seen church members crippled when their worlds crumbled. How sad that any daughter of God would suffer unnecessarily! Not knowing God intimately is a monumental disadvantage when disaster strikes. Wouldn't you rather be the one who understands where her hope lies? It's in the one you claim to believe: "Be strong and courageous. Do not be terrified; do not be discouraged, for the Lord your God will be with you wherever you go" (Joshua 1:9).

Are you able to claim the Father's promises when life is difficult? Do you believe he is there, loving you in the midst of the crisis? Total reliance is a pretty tall order, that's for sure, and one that requires spiritual maturity. But after you walk with him awhile—after you truly develop a heart for the Father—then your belief will spill over in these ways:

• Crying out to God will be ongoing.
• Discerning evil will be empowering.
• Feeling the Spirit will be encouraging.
• Reading Scripture will be satisfying.
• Remembering his faithfulness will be rewarding.

Life can throw some pretty hard curve balls, but believe in your God anyway. He is truly the Father who holds you up and calms you down. And his magnificent presence, the one that obliterates anything this world throws our way, is convincingly real. I can feel it. I can see it. I know it in my heart. Amen! Thank you, Father!

Want to Dig Deeper?

Even the Old Testament prophets got discouraged with this evil world, and Elijah was no different. God had just performed a miracle, but soon after that, Elijah's life was in danger. (Talk about ups and downs!) Read 1 Kings 19:1–11 to see how the Father took special care of his discouraged but obedient child.

_____

_____

_____

_____

Day Five: Love Him with Your Heart

For the past six weeks, we've done some soul searching, to say the least, exploring God and our desire for him. Hopefully, you not only know *about* him but you *know* him. I pray that you are humbled and awed by the heavenly Father. And because he loved you first, the only response that makes sense is loving him back. Since the study began, can you say that your relationship with God has reached a deeper closeness? If so, then write a brief prayer of commitment to him:

Yes, our hearts should be turned toward God, but do you ever consider just how much his own heart is bursting with love for us? Even though I've known the Lord for many years, the kindness he shows me is still overwhelming. Read these verses about God's intense love for you, his precious daughter:

- "He tends his flock like a shepherd: He gathers the lambs in his arms and carries them close to his heart; He gently leads those that have young" (Isaiah 40:11).
- "[Jesus said], I give them eternal life, and they shall never perish; no one can snatch them out of my hand. My Father, who has given them to me, is greater than all; no one can snatch them out of my Father's hand" (John 10:28–29).

1. What part of God's description as a shepherd is especially touching to you?

---

2. How do you respond, knowing that he holds you tightly and securely?

What a powerful love affair! God, the one who has every right to roll his eyes at my pitiful self, loves me with the tenderness of a caring shepherd. And those mighty hands, the same hands that created green pastures, hold me closely, away from harm. He holds you too if you belong to him. Don't you want to sing from the mountaintops or drop to your knees in praise? The Father of creation has a tender heart for you!

The only logical response, in my humble opinion, is to return the favor. And boy, am I determined to do so! Even though my human heart is limited, I pray that every beat echoes his. Even though my hands have sinned, they are raised toward heaven. And even though my life is short, I want every breath to praise his name. This passage in Psalm 91 helps me understand the rewards and the responsibilities of pure devotion:

> "Because he loves me," says the Lord, "I will rescue him; I will protect him, for he acknowledges my name. He will call upon me, and I will answer him; I will be with him in trouble, I will deliver him and honor him. With long life will I satisfy him and show him my salvation."
>
> Psalm 91:14–16

1. What does God promise you, his devoted child?

_____

_____

2. Why does God promise these things to you?

_____

_____

3. What does a passage like this reveal about God's heart for you?

_____

_____

This study is complete, but your growing relationship with the Father has only just begun. As much as you love him now, imagine how much more there is to experience! And the key to getting there, precious daughter of God, is by keeping a close eye on what matters most: "Above all else, guard your heart, for it is the wellspring of life" (Proverbs 4:23). Are you ready for the next step in your spiritual journey? Today, pray that with each new day, your heart grows ever stronger and purer, looking more and more like his.

Want to Dig Deeper?

The Bible has a lot to say about healthy spiritual hearts, but it also describes how they should *not* function. Read Hebrews 3:7–13, and list the symptoms of a sick, sinful heart. How would you describe your own heart for God?

_____

_____

_____

_____

Afterword

If you're reading this book, chances are you're interested in learning more about the Father. You believe he exists, and you'd like to know him better. You might even love him. If so, do you realize that God loved you first? The Bible says that even before you were born, he lovingly formed everything about you: body, spirit, soul, and potential. And he couldn't wait to spend every minute with you. Why? Because he was—and still is—so completely in love with you!

There's a problem, though: As much as God loves you, he hates sin. And because you've messed up at some point in your life (so have I), the ugliness of that sin separates you from God's perfect, holy character. So how can a situation like this—a broken relationship—be restored? That's where Jesus Christ comes in. Because God loves you so much, he sent his perfect son to pay the cost of every sin. And the cost was great: Jesus gave his life on a cross to pay for every mistake you would ever make. And then when he arose out of that tomb three days later, the penalty of sin and separation from God were gone forever. All for you. And me. And for any person who believes.

So how can you develop a close relationship with the Father? All you have to do is accept this gift of God's Son, just like I did as an eight-year-old. Believe in the reason for his death and resurrection, and then follow his example of honoring God. It's a miraculous gift. It's an intentional decision. And, as I've found, it's a lifelong commitment. Here are some passages from the Bible that explain a believer's forgiven, secure, and treasured relationship with Holy God:

- "God so loved the world that he gave his one and only son, that whoever believes in him shall not perish but have eternal life" (John 3:16).
- "Jesus answered, 'I am the way and the truth and the life. No one comes to the Father except through me. If you really knew me, you would know my Father as well. From now on, you do know him and have seen him'" (John 14:6–7).

- "God is light. In him there is no darkness at all. If we claim to have fellowship with him yet walk in the darkness, we lie and do not live by the truth. But if we walk in the light, as he is in the light, we have fellowship with one another, and the blood of Jesus, his son, purifies us from all sin. If we claim to be without sin, we deceive ourselves, and the truth is not in us. If we confess our sins, he is faithful and just and will forgive us our sins and purify us from all unrighteousness" (1 John 1:5–9).

If you'd like more information on Jesus's loving sacrifice, then please talk with your youth director or pastor. Or contact me personally at www.avasturgeon.com. I'd love to talk with you about the gift of Christ, a loving relationship with God, and your life of incredible purpose.

Leader's Guide

A Note from the Author

Dear Adult Leader,

What a blessing you are to a grateful group of young women! Whether you're facilitating a few high schoolers or a packed house of college students, they can't wait to discover God with their peers. And they're just as excited about getting to know you! Are you a little unsure about all this? I usually am, but each time a new group starts, I'm always relieved that students simply crave authenticity, love, and one-on-one attention. And with God's help, I can fill that order. So can you!

I've included some ideas for each weekly meeting, but feel free to tweak away, especially after observing your particular group's personality. The main goal, I believe, is helping each participant feel comfortable sharing her struggles and victories, all while receiving biblical truth. If you'd like to contact me when your study begins, just e-mail me at avasturge@yahoo.com. It would be a privilege to lift up you and your students to the Father.

Blessings,

Ava Sturgeon

A Word to the Wise

1. Length of study

   - Even though *A Daughter's Heart* is divided into six weeks of study, consider the book as an eight-week venture. Use the first week to distribute books, complete the introductory section, and explain the format. Use the last week as a celebration time of testimonies, food, and fun.
   - Weekly meetings should last between sixty and ninety minutes, depending on the time frame for snacks and fellowship. Each chapter discussion averages forty-five minutes to an hour.

2. Materials

Each participant will need her own book, Bible, pen, and personal notebook (optional). Leaders will need to keep extra materials on hand, including an additional book or two, for latecomers to the study.

3. Room setup

Because the study is discussion-based, the location should be cozy and comfortable. Consider meeting at someone's home or in a room with large throw pillows or chairs arranged in a circle.

4. Student enrollment

- Since you'll purchase books ahead of time, pre-enrollment is necessary. Ideally, when students arrive for the first introductory meeting, they will receive their books.
- Some groups cut off enrollment at ten or twelve so that the size remains intimate. Others prefer unlimited enrollment with plans to break into smaller groups during discussion time. Keep in mind that this setup requires several adult leaders.

5. Leaders' responsibilities

Think of yourself as a facilitator, helping participants stay on topic and discover biblical truths for themselves. Here are some tips that help me guide young women:

- Complete each lesson for yourself in order to select topics for deeper discussions.
- Make time for one-on-one talks with participants. They will know that you care specifically for them, and you'll get an idea of where they are spiritually.
- Assure participants that each session is a safe place to ask questions, vent frustrations, or reveal struggles. Ask the group of make a pact of confidentiality.
- Report any serious issues, such as allegations of abuse, to your youth director, minister, or government agency.
- Pray for each student. Ask God to prepare her heart, as well as yours.

A Plan in Place

Introductory session

1. Have a sign-in area to pick up books, complete information cards, and receive nametags. (Heart-shaped named tags emphasize the theme of falling in love with the Father.)
2. For snacks related to the theme, consider Hershey's kisses and heart-shaped cookies.
3. While early birds wait for the session to begin, assign the following activity: Discuss the differences between infatuation ("I've got a crush!") and true love ("I'm in love!"). Ask students to work together and record their thoughts on poster board that you've prepared beforehand.
4. Begin the study by discussing students' thoughts on infatuation and love. Guide the conversation toward God's commitment to his daughters. Which category resembles his commitment to us? Ask someone to read aloud 1 John 4:7–10. Brainstorm ways in which God loves us unconditionally.
5. Ask students to consider for themselves the theme of this study: "Are you in love with the Father, or are you infatuated?" (Look at the lists again.) "How can you fall in lasting love with God?" (By getting to know him. *That's* the purpose of this book.)
6. Open books to the introductory session, "Recognizing Where You Are." As they follow along, read the first three paragraphs, pausing to let participants answer and discuss the questions. After reading Psalm 63:1–8, ask them to complete the rest of the introduction individually.
7. When most are finished, direct them to the "What's Next?" portion at the end of the session. Read the directions, making sure they understand the importance of completing one lesson/devotion a day. Encourage students to mark their books as they read, underlining or highlighting anything that catches their eye.
8. Ask for prayer requests. Then break into pairs for a time of prayer, asking God to bless the next few weeks of study.

Week 1: Comprehending Who He Is

1. Icebreaker: In small groups of two or three, ask young women to describe God to someone who's never heard of him. Provide paper and markers, instructing them to create a poster that "advertises" the Father. They may draw, write words and phrases,

or include Bible verses. Then after ten minutes or so, encourage each group to share their work.

2. As the study begins, ask participants to consider what the world thinks of God's character. Contrast the world's view of God with the beliefs of loving daughters.

3. Discuss each lesson/devotion from week one. Each student should have her book open, ready to weigh in on the topics she's been contemplating. During this first week of discussion, students may be hesitant to speak up. That's okay; just guide them through each lesson, making sure to reference scripture and ask their thoughts about some general questions.

4. When all five lessons/devotions have been discussed, encourage each participant to think about which trait of God means the most to her. Why this particular trait? If your group is already comfortable and transparent, then ask students which trait of God they most often take for granted. What steps can they take to correct this?

5. For next week, make sure participants know to complete all five lessons/devotions for week two. Assign each lesson for next week to several students, challenging them to discuss interesting points with the entire group during the upcoming meeting.

6. Spend time in prayer, concentrating on praise and thanksgiving for the character of God.

Week 2: Appreciating What He Did

1. Icebreaker: Praise songs about Jesus are fitting for this week's discussion, as well as a brief scene from *The Passion of the Christ* (The movie is quite violent, so consider your audience. The scene on the cross just before Jesus dies would work for most participants.). You might also create a blank timeline of Jesus's life, encouraging students as a group to complete it.

2. As the study begins, ask students to explain how Jesus fits into their loving relationship with God. (The whole reason for Christ's sacrifice was to make our relationship with God possible. Jesus also gave us the perfect example of how to love and honor the Father.)

3. Discuss each lesson/devotion from week two. Each participant should have her book open, ready to contribute. If you assigned specific girls for lessons last week, then ask them to mention thoughts or passages that caught their attention. After they've shared, open up the discussion to everyone else. Continue this

strategy until all five lessons/devotions for the week have been explored.

4. Ask young women to answer this question: What can Jesus's life on earth teach us about our own relationships with God?

5. For the next meeting, make sure participants know to complete week three. Assign each lesson to several students ahead of time, encouraging them to discuss interesting points within the lesson with the entire group next week.

6. End in a time of prayer, thanking Jesus for his sacrifice, as well as thanking the Father for providing a way for continued relationship with him.

Week 3: Embracing What He Promises

1. Icebreaker: Read a copy of the traditional wedding vows aloud, asking students to comment on the promises that are most important to them. Have one student list on poster board the promises that spouses make to each other. Keep it visible during the entire session.

2. Remind participants that daughters of God are also brides of Christ. Read Revelation 19:7. What promises in the traditional wedding vows are also true of the commitments that God makes to his children? Consult the list of promises for reference.

3. Discuss each lesson/devotion from week three. Each participant should have her book open, ready to contribute. If you assigned lessons last week, then begin with day one, asking them to mention thoughts or passages that caught their attention. After they've shared, open up the discussion to everyone else. Continue this strategy until all five lessons/devotions for the week have been explored.

4. Ask young women to answer this question aloud: As you think of God's promises to you, what promises should you make to God? Give each participant a sheet of paper and ask her to write a love letter to the Father, renewing her commitment to the relationship. Let students take these letters home as reminders of their commitment.

5. For the next meeting, make sure participants know to complete week four. Ask five students to lead a particular lesson/devotion next week. If you don't get enough volunteers, then pair up the assignments.

6. End with sentence prayers, asking each participant to thank God for a particular promise.

Week 4: Understanding What He Wants

1. Icebreaker: Ask several students to share how God has become more real to them over the past few weeks. Assure them that he wants to know them more and more. Then play a reflective Christian song (artists such as Chris Tomlin and Mercy Me come to mind) as they kneel and talk with the Father, praying for devotion in their hearts, minds, and actions.
2. Place these words around the room: reverence, praise, gratitude, obedience, and loyalty. Ask students which is toughest for them to give God. Whatever word seems to be a popular choice, start the discussion with the coinciding lesson/devotion. Then choose another and so on until all the lessons/devotions have been explored. (Yes, the topic discussions for this week will be "out of order" in relation to the book.) If individual students volunteered to lead specific lessons, let them guide the conversation (you'll be ready to jump in when needed).
3. When all five lessons/devotions have been discussed, ask each young woman to answer these questions aloud: Which of God's desires is easiest for a new Christian? Why? Which of God's desires becomes easier the longer you've been following him? Why?
4. For the next meeting, make sure participants know to complete week five. Ask for five volunteers to lead a particular lesson/devotion next week. If you don't get enough offers, then pair up the assignments.
5. End with your prayer over the students, letting them hear your intercession for their pure, devoted hearts.

Week 5: Acknowledging What He Conquers

1. Icebreaker: Have computer paper and markers available. As each student arrives, instruct her to take a sheet of paper and list several struggles girls face. Then ask her to circle the most frustrating struggle. When everyone has finished, encourage participants to share their answers. Ask young women to read Ephesians 6:10–13. Remind them that struggles are ploys of Satan, but God's children are conquerors. Tell them to stand, wad up their papers, and to step on them. Then throw away the struggles as a symbolic gesture of victory.

2. Ask young women which specific lesson/devotion struck a chord with them. Whatever topic seems to be a popular choice, start the discussion with the coinciding lesson/devotion. Then choose another and so on until all the lessons/devotions have been explored. If individual students volunteered to lead specific lessons, then let them facilitate, knowing that you'll come to their aid when needed.

3. Ask these questions: Which of these struggles are the most difficult for young women? Why? How can each struggle negatively affect the way you view God?

4. For the next meeting, make sure participants know to complete week six. Tell them that they will lead the entire discussion as a group, so ask them to highlight interesting or challenging passages for each lesson/devotion.

5. Pair each student with someone with whom she's not particularly close. Instruct each pair to share a struggle and then to pray specifically about each struggle.

Week 6: Believing What He Says

1. Icebreaker: Ask the young women to list reasons why believers turn away from God. Then discuss real-life scenarios in which people have clung to their faith despite difficult times. (If you find local anecdotes to this effect, this week's topic will take on a personal touch.) Consider why years of loving God ensures a solid faith, even during difficulty.

2. Instruct students to begin their discussion with the lesson that caught their attention most. Then sit back, allowing them to move from one topic to the next. Of course, add direction when necessary, but aim for peer discussion in which they are "feeding themselves."

3. When all five lessons/devotions have been discussed, ask these questions: How will you keep your faith in God strong when troubles come? When trouble comes, how will you feel the Father's love?

4. For next week, plan a celebration time. Encourage several students who have grown spiritually during the Bible study to share their experiences. Assign a participant to plan games, and ask others to organize and provide refreshments.

5. Pair each young woman with someone with whom she's not particularly close. Instruct each pair to pray specifically for each other, asking for unwavering faith no matter what.

Closing Session: Celebration

In my experience, young women have a lot to say at the ends of studies like these, and you'll want to hear their testimonies of spiritual growth. Planning a time for this allows students to talk without being rushed during regular study sessions. You could plan a whole "love theme," asking them to wear red, write love notes of encouragement for each other, etc. Just have a good time, celebrating the abiding love of God. (And if you'd like, e-mail me after your session is over so that I can praise God along with you!)

Do You Know Your Worth?

A Daughter's Worth, Ava Sturgeon's debut Bible study, explores the beautiful value of God's children, no matter what the world says. And, as readers discover, worthy daughters want nothing more than to please their heavenly Father. It's a twelve-week study, perfect for young women thirteen and up who face the following issues:

- Accepting the Father's love
- Embracing true beauty
- Managing emotions
- Choosing good friends
- Treasuring the family
- Dating with discretion
- Finding God at school
- Living with purpose

Visit www.avasturgeon.com or www.tatepublishing.com for ordering information.